Blind Date

Blind Date

Sex and Philosophy

ANNE DUFOURMANTELLE

❦ ❦ ❦

Translated from the French by Catherine Porter
Introduction by Avital Ronell

University of Illinois Press
Urbana and Chicago

Ouvrage publié avec le concours du Ministère français
chargé de la culture—Centre national du livre.

The publisher gratefully acknowledges that this work is
published with the assistance of the French Ministry of
Culture—the National Centre of the Book.

Library of Congress Cataloging-in-Publication Data
Dufourmantelle, Anne.
[Blind date. English]
Blind date : sex and philosophy / Anne Dufourmantelle ;
translated from the French by Catherine Porter ;
introduction by Avital Ronell.
p.   cm.
Includes bibliographical references and index.
ISBN-13 978-0-252-03263-9 (cloth : alk. paper)
ISBN-10 0-252-03263-2 (cloth : alk. paper)
ISBN-13 978-0-252-07488-2 (pbk. : alk. paper)
ISBN-10 0-252-07488-2 (pbk. : alk. paper)
1. Sex—Philosophy. I. Title.
HQ21.D84   2007
306.701—dc22   2007015799

To Mali Ston,
Tadussack,
and Songs

To live—that means for us to change all that we are, constantly, into light and flame . . . that art of transfiguration—that is philosophy.

—Nietzsche

From what star have we fallen together here?

—Nietzsche to Lou, the first time he saw her

Contents

Introduction:
The Stealth Pulse of Philosophy

Avital Ronell

Philosophy has never gone to bed. Commanding the most recondite corners of experience, philosophy regulates the phenomenal intensit-ies of the days and nights of sheer wonder. Hegel billed it as PG-18 or, according to his scorecard, as a distinctly adult form of exertion—"for adults only"— philosophy, ever mature and self-knowing, has never shaken its childlike appeal.

Once in a while, the naive, fresh look by which it is recognized appears to be a specialty of the house, even if the clean-cut hale proves to be familiar with more hardened maneuvers, such as sublation or rupture or proliferating probability theorems or feisty critical flips. Whether scouring a sizable range of empirical urgencies or stretching the speculative account, whether scanning a grammar, subduing an unruly logic, or tallying phrasal injuries, the philosophical advance, no matter how limited or restricted to its own sense of partial object, evinces a totalizing impulse. There is a flavor of innocence to its expansionist instincts, its adolescent will to dominate and childlike control over the incalculable. The winner, in any case, takes all—or, more ethically inflected, philosophy, in its grownup stages, is responsible for nearly anything that happens or fails to happen under its supervision, including that which has nothing at all to do with logical subdivisions of event and statement. Philosophy remains responsible for the inexhaustible spectrum of things or nonthings that dwell in its vicinity, for their descriptions and redescriptions, their abrupt emergence or essential lapses, their unforeseen yet inescapable residue: This involves a lot of work, covering a lot of ground, not to mention the span of groundlessness that philosophy obligates itself to clear, each time anew, according to ever more trying protocols for seizing the day.

Philosophy has never gone to bed. Restive and worn, philosophy has kept itself up at night—watching, deliberating, phenomenalizing the vital nocturnal expanse. No matter how straight edged or analytical, empirically fitted or mathematically nailed, it hangs on to the traces of an originating breach: conceived in awe and given over to stupor, philosophy can pry out the intricate webs of existence and tear up even the most subphenomenal ranges of intentional meaning. Still, something is missing in the vocabulary of a relentless probe—something that remains emphatically unsaid or, at least, unpronounceable in all its languages and idioms. On this point it is hard to understand whether the philosophical capacity for knowledge or inquiry is stopped short by a wave of superiority, worn down by impatient irritation, or flustered by the blush of modesty—a mood or mode hard to collate with the dominant tones of philosophical positing. Whatever the cause or hidden power play, something has systematically slipped out of the articulated philosophical reach for being. In the film *Derrida*, the eponymous protagonist says at one point that he would like to have known what Hegel had to say about sex; or rather, if memory serves, what Hegel would have written about his sex life. No: he said, I think, that he wanted to *know* about Hegel's sex life. He could have asked for anything at that moment of the filmed interview, but the category of unknowability fell to "sex." To Hegel and sex, ewww.

Anne Dufourmantelle, best known in the English-only world for the volume she published with Jacques Derrida, *Of Hospitality*, initiates a spectacular exploration of the wish, half-seriously expressed by Derrida, for something that I might call, in his spirit and on his epistemological watch, carnalphallogocentrism knowing. A practicing psychoanalyst, substantial philosopher, and acquisitions editor at the notable Éditions Stock in Paris, Anne Dufourmantelle opens the dossier on a history of philosophy's phobic flight by arranging a meeting between an immense philosophical corpus and its evaded counterpart or sometime mirror and silent partner: "sex." The meeting, which may or may not take place—everything conspires against it—resembles a blind date, which is to say that two undisclosed identities or in fact two nonidentities are asked to give each other a chance to yield a shared moment, if only for the purpose of sizing each other up and attempting to match and project compatibilities. What astonishes Dufourmantelle is that the two have not yet met or said they've met, but require that arrangements be made for a world-historical tryout. Blind yet trusting, each party seems to back away from the embarrassment of an arranged encounter and its desperate implications. The intrusive and violent nature of a somewhat coerced meeting reflects the practice of sexual exclusion to which philosophy to this day or date remains party, at least in terms of the verifiability of its historical dossiers and logical protocols. Philosophy, which encrypts love in its very name, covers the origin as sex or sex as amorous brace and origin, without necessarily pulling up a moralizing diction and other simply repressive maneuvers. Still, they are closer to each other than we may think.

Both sex and philosophy share the jubilation of being, the abandonment to the abandon of beings that in the end can claim no object. Sex has no object—there may be no such thing as sexual relations, as Lacan conclusively observed—and philosophy suffers considerably from its lack of object, as Dufourmantelle demonstrates. Both sex and philosophy tend to get organized around a concept of lack, something that motivates parallel runs of probing and plugging that help to make up acts of questioning. Still, sex never arouses a question for philosophy, which abounds in love, friendship, perjury dialogue, straying, *Sorge*, convergence, conversation, and the occasional caress. "Sex is the silent other of philosophy," writes Dufourmantelle, "which nonetheless has given itself the task of thinking being in its entirety," leaving nothing, in principle, out of bounds.

All the same, philosophy has hosted prize orgies. From Plato to Patočka, sex has been metonymized into *furor* and episodes of self-splitting ravishment. Dionysian raves have defined the breaking limits of passion since the god Dionysus served up ecstasy and shattered all self-identical molds. Part demon, part man, part god, he is pursued by the goddess Hera, who wants his hide because he persistently subverts the order of the living and the dead, rubbing out memory and introducing, in the dimension of tragedy and passing through the corridors of Pan, all manner of excess, obscenity, erotic overkill. In the discordant and dismembering movement of the Dionysian dance, the ancient Greeks put up a body that, when ripping itself apart, exposes truth to disfigurement, hurling away that which separates death from life, memory from futurity, representation from desire. The body evinces a scream, flushing and flashing blood, searing flesh, attaching to the entrails of a matriciel origin and generation. Dionysus never steers clear of danger and retains his status of dangerous god to the extent that he remains a stranger to a world ordered by *logos*. The bodily pleasure that this god commands, the intoxicating suspension of recognizable determinations and fixable limits, has Dionysus on the most-wanted list because, to the extent that he's still on the loose, philosophy runs the major risk of seeing truth despoiled. Still beating, the Dionysian pulse continues to be felt in the most austere precincts of philosophical reflection.

❧ ❧ ❧ Philosophy has never gone to bed. It pulses with daybreak, forgetting itself each morning in the agony of an original becoming. Obsessed with origin, being turns away from the origin, as Hölderlin famously noted, though he was clearly going with another flow, drafting a different thought of the forgotten origin and repelled source (*Urquelle*). Attuned to an urgent and originary forgetting, Hölderlin's language traveled the limit of poetic witnessing and finished up by donating a way of seeing, "a third eye," to the philosophical probe. The split over the origin was henceforth a matter of shared custody. Let me now try to determine the standout qualities of an often stealth alliance between the philosophical interrogation and the poetic gaze.

It would be best first to review the internal split that governs the scene of our inquiry—the state of exception that philosophy harbors within itself, over which it divides its most crucially diverted properties, ceaselessly in dispute. According to the work before us, the fate of thinking is bound up in the impossible relation to "sex" that philosophy, in its own dispossessing way, maintains. Prompted by anxiety and insomnia—native to the figure of thinking—philosophy indulges recognizable behaviors of denial and falsification: Skirting the issue of sexuated being, it has disabled a vital meter of finitude. To the extent that sexuality signals another way of drumming up the hold of mortality, it belongs to any credible thinking of the limits of life and must respond to such crises as accompany the finite markers of being. Philosophy, for the most part, has come clean on the pressure zones of finite being, yet it has persistently skipped a beat, leaving sex, at best, to while in remote spaces that quietly host the compatible themes of sacrifice and bestiality—the often disinherited precincts of philosophical reflection. Still, philosophy nears its forbidden object and has provided that *eros* and *logos* be propelled by the same movement of life, invention, creativity—by the same movement based on the *passion* of ignorance. To a certain extent, philosophy does not in the end want to know about desire and its messy entrapments or returns to childhood. On the whole, philosophy, whether entrusted to Plato or Hegel and their specific offshoots, remains a matter mostly for the older crowd and their high-tech screening devices.

Philosophy has never gone to bed. This assertion may explain in part the insistent tropes of weariness and the marks of sheer fatigue to which Lévinas and Blanchot revert in their philosophical expositions. Vigilant and sleepless, philosophy, for the most part, has been too high to get it on. According to Dufourmantelle, a critical pileup of phobic anxieties, fear, and exiles has prevented philosophy from keeping the appointment with a decisive inflection of its origin. This centuries-long avoidance strategy has implications for our destiny. Why would "sex" belong to what I would call an "obliterature," the space of thinking's disavowal? Maybe it's due in part to the cult of solitude, the contemplative cast of philosophical inquiry; maybe it's because Socrates' wife was ugly; maybe they practice an ethics of sublimation that prompts them to dance, to walk, to keep floating in the middle of the lake near Geneva; maybe they were always already throttled by the ends of man or the last man and waiting out the dawn of the trans-human, announced at the end of philosophy by Nietzsche. Whatever the reason, if it's a matter of reason, philosophy cleared the deck when it came to handling sex. Yet as anyone who has survived the twentieth century knows, the abomination or mere "forgetting" of sex also provides a smoking gun: The effort of deletion indicates a storehouse of untapped language, protecting the repressive recesses of a persistent divide.

At the same time and posed with a slight difference, it could well be that philosophy has only ever engaged in sexual practice, even if this engagement assumed the occasional forms of shadowboxing or enacted the gravitas of parallel play and figural dissembling. Philosophy's relation to modalities of bliss and desire, and their requisite deflections beneath or beyond the pleasure principle, are legion. Philosophy's effort to know the language and limits of bodies and their attendant affects, instinctual plunges, inscriptive migrations, or sensuous mobility has been on the rise in the time zone linking Plato to Wittgenstein. Even rolling back—or ahead, depending on the standpoint from which one philosophizes—to the innovative supplement of "disinterested pleasure," one finds the eighteenth century struggling with a purposeful anxiety around the supposition of discernable delight. Among so many other things, *The Critique of Judgment* appears to confer a needed breathing space from the pressures of privative attachment, scaling the heights of need, possession, and object propulsion. It is as if, through Kant, philosophy might have called for a time-out—a ploy that Nietzsche in turn blackballed and, in any case, scorned. Kant secured a site for a kind of wildlife preserve, clearing a space for the harmonious interplay of the faculties when touched by the beautiful form; or rather, when precisely *not* touched but stirred—maybe called or sparked, but certainly not touched. Nietzsche didn't see cause for the Kantian chastity belt, for the desexualized drought that the Third Critique forecast. Still, Nietzsche, for his part, did not say or use "sex" to score his point or motivate his stylus; he just laughed out loud at the old man and warned against the global billing for which Kant took credit.

❧ ❧ ❧ In recent decades, we've been alerted to the furtive encounters, illicit contingencies, or highly invested swap meets that traverse modernity, stylizing the different strokes of philosophy in the bedroom. Never very far from contemporary appraisals of sexuality on the make, Bataille pornographized the *cogito,* Kathy Acker ran up a bill of theoretical excess, and, nowadays, Dennis Cooper convokes Nietzsche babies zoned out and unable to command their libidinal trust funds. Poetry has always stood in for sensual rapture and continues to drive the scansion of sexual appetite. From the Greek, Sanskrit, and Persian fragments through the immortal Catullus, to Goethe's "Roman Elegies," to contemporary poetry's abundant and intimate pilgrimages to all uncensored languages, genders, and bodies, poetry mantles itself in affirming promiscuity or the linguistic ardor of erotic pursuit. The now familiar crossovers into philosophical territory, for which I have provisionally recruited the names Bataille, Acker, and Cooper, meet a different fate, however. Their philosophical raids end, for the most part, in detention centers where philosophy holds back the largely literary culprits that have stepped up sexualized reflection.

Closely tied to the mores of contemporary writers, Friedrich Schlegel to this day takes beatings from philosophical overlords who continue to press charges against the philosophical pornography machine, the *pornosophy,* that his novel *Lucinde* indulges. As Paul de Man once drove home, the scandal of Schlegel consists in the crossover of genres, the wanton staging of incompatible codes, and the ensuing contaminations of reciprocally alien formalities rather than in the buildup of any specific or accreditable content. These writers, including, of course, the formidable Marquis de Sade, have tried to take philosophy to bed. But even with Socrates lurking in the men's room of certain banquet halls and Lyotard's truck with the libidinal economy, philosophy, as a discipline and strongly determined type of reflection, would not hear of it. No one, not even those who put their bodies on the line or wriggled around like Nietzsche, admitted sex—or their own perhaps citable or excitable relation to sex—into the backrooms of philosophical speculation. Philosophy, however, prides itself on taking hold of life and exploring its various articulations. Why this unabating level of discretion or self-censorship?

❧ ❧ ❧ Sometimes a pulse is missing. In Eastern medicines, the depths and rhythms of several pulses are routinely tapped in order to gauge the health of a living body. Some of these pulses can be weaker than others, and some supersede others in terms of the vitalities on which they report and the collapse they predict. However, Western medicine, not far from decisive monotheistic habits, tends to focus in on one pulse, crowding out the subtle varieties of signs and linkups to which the body has recourse when betraying its bustling itineraries. Even a locution such as "*the* body" reveals a mostly Western bias, since ayurveda, for instance, tallies up ten bodies and counting. Be that as it may, even when limited to the domain of one body on which it scans, fixes, staggers, or sublimates, Western philosophy has a tendency to keep a lid on the id, bag the body, and repeal the horizon of ecstatic abandon—or, let us say, it keeps one or two windows in the range of ecstatic abandon resolutely shuttered. It is perhaps no mere coincidence that non-Western medical practices come from a climate that frequently supports the multiplicity of bodies that exercise their abundant rights based on the claims of energetic or subtle being, including those promoted by and inclusive of the *Kama Sutra.*

On the Western front (though it is senseless to suppose that cross-overs and significant incursions have not had their day—senseless to suppose that East and West do not live, as in fact they now must, by reciprocal contamination), the body has been singularized and kicked to the philosophical curb. With the body, and especially with its erogenous zoning ordinances, something has been systematically abandoned, leaving a shutter or shudder that resembles traumatic opening and indicates the material self-exceeding of the body's relation to itself. This is one indication for referencing the way body makes itself happen, with or without different levers of consciousness, with or without relation, with or without philosophy and its fateful arbitration.

❧ ❧ ❧ The studied aversion of the philosophical gaze to sex is the subject of this book. However, it is not clear that sex claims object status in or "outside" of philosophy, or that something like sex is at all something to be *seen* by a practice so ocularcentric as gazing or by internally installed viewers such as, say, intuition. In some sense *Blind Date* traces the history of an aversion that monitors the constantly rebounding intrusion of an expelled negativity. Under censorship and whited out by the blinding light of surveillance, "sex" constitutes a site of massive distortion where philosophy seeks truth. This is where philosophy falters, trips over itself as it endeavors to establish the rectitude of its search. To love and to probe are related activities whose connection philosophy must sever in order to proceed. With sex in philosophical lockup, part of an inexplicable run for cover and tactical dissimulation, how does it stand with philosophy's relation to truth? Has an essential aspect, the very integrity of relentless philosophical investigation, been impugned? What has become of "Our Probity!," as Kant cried out and Nancy scrupulously interpreted? More historico-anthropologically profiled, what are we to make of the sexually invested lineup or erotic transfer stations beginning with Socrates' boys to the X-rated correspondence posted between Martin Heidegger and Hannah Arendt? Are they off or on the charts of philosophical inquiry? Where on the mapping of philosophical *Einstellung* or attitude does the material interpretation of love, *philo*, get situated?

Anne Dufourmantelle, who sees philosophical essence as another name for *jouissance,* marking the jubilation of being diffused along the body, considers that philosophical experience, like the sexual act or mystical transport, has for its principal task the effort desperately to approach a lacking object, to bear down on what is missing within a happening momentum. Unaccounted for, something remains rigorously inappropriable in the very movement of appropriation. In this way the thought of essence closes in on Bataille's rendering of an "experience without experience." These efforts at mooring—whether in fact effortless, strained, or simply missed—spin around an ungraspable axis that holds together extreme limits of experience, casting the traumatic shadow of eventfulness on the naming of sex in philosophy.

Although unannounced within traditional philosophical protocols, sex has nonetheless dispatched its discursive emissaries and envoys, consistently realigning representative decoys that remain linked to their home base. On the whole, philosophy has refrained from naming sex, sticking close in this regard to its home-base ascetic ideals. True, Kierkegaard came out with his seduction manual. Yet he took Schlegel to task for crossing over to pulp with *Lucinde.* And sometimes philosophy introduces props, which is what prompted Lacan to present his famous essay "Kant with Sade." Lacan declines to give the title simply as "Kant *and* Sade" but places Kant *with* Sade. As with Heidegger, Nancy, and Derrida, the *with* is crucial for thinking predication or reviewing newly cut angles of *Mitsein*—the "being-with" that reassigns the place of the Subject in philosophical thought. From instances of "being-with" that splice sexualized proximities to the *il y a* or the *es gibt* that establishes—or, in the case of Lacan, destabilizes—sexual relations, we are dealt a vocabulary that tries to tap into the recesses and binding qualities of shared being. (Evidently, his famous "il n'y a pas" of sexual relations has put me, like others, into severe repetition compulsion: so, *encore,* sex does not relate.) How tight is one with the other, what are the limits or ecstasies of this being-with that may or fails to relate? To a certain extent, Dufourmantelle engages the unrelatable primer of thought by conjugating philosophy with sex.

As said, there has been no lack of envoys or decoys to stand in and stand by for sex, and literature has often been responsible for crashing the gates of straight-edged parties. It is as if philosophy always had a bed ready for its unannounced night visitors. But nothing much has happened. Or we haven't yet heard about it, not more substantially than the rumor of what happened at the all-nighter, the banquet thrown by Socrates. Dufourmantelle, for her part, can do little more than arrange an encounter, set up the blind date of two hapless yet readied entities. For her, the encounter requires that a place be made for the other who infinitely exceeds the place where one awaits. To give oneself over to philosophy is to ready one's being, embrace a quest, often a quest for truth that resembles a chase. One is "in pursuit," one hunts down the object of desire. The sexual encounter cointricates with thought: "tous les dialogues de Platon en témoignent:" Plato's Dialogues testify to this fact in their entirety (43). Truth, object of voracious pursuit, is a pathology, "une passion maladive," of metaphysics and thus in human drivenness (24). But some types of pathological excess are necessary for life and prompt creative breakthrough. Nietzsche's passionate relation to truth sets it off as a necessary illusion. Close on this point to *thinking,* sex engages a certain sensuality of illusion. On another but related register, Dufourmantelle introduces the notion of *kairòs,* the here and now absolutely deployed, the instant of decision or, for Homer and Sophocles, the moment when the archer hits the opponent's heart, indicating precise targeting, the right moment—the hit after which everything turns around. Ungraspable by nature, it meets the target without offering a sense of what has really happened. Sex, remarks Dufourmantelle, may be another mask of *kairòs*.

The emphatically targeted-and-missed moments of *kairòs* collide with traumatic precision, for sex in or as philosophy refuses presentation without ever having left the scene yet keeps recurring, we can say with some certainty, on an invisible channel that parasites every philosophical work. Some of these works shake off their parasites, others host them; still others panic and put out an apotropaic semiotic to subdue the unwelcome intrusion. For the most part, sex annuls as it presents itself as exposition, scheme, or theme, leaving an unreadable residue as its calling card. "It" arrives at the place of an incessant vanishing point. . . . Still and again: What is sex? Does it have an essence, carry a truth; can it bring to term the tiniest of concepts? Or is it the startup engine for elegant neurotic symptomatologies and their neighboring hysterical dialect, to which we owe the scientific impulse, artistic outbursts, philosophical systematizations and other manmade defenses or hostile grammars? Is sex even "natural"?

Dufourmantelle writes that everything is owed to sex. In the next sentence she avers that nothing is owed to sex, thus canceling the debt on which a massive table of calculations has been tallied up. What does it mean to owe so much that the very notion of indebtedness bellies up? I'm not sure that we can count on me to figure this out. What could be said beyond establishing the simple recap of a self-surpassing economy or a reversion to the gift giving of the *es gibt*, the *il y a*, or even the gift of death of which our teachers have written, saying something rather than nothing about the generosity of being—a generosity that, according to Dufourmantelle, would not refrain from admitting to the thought of engendering exuberance.

❦ ❦ ❦ So. Maybe you have to take my introduction on blind faith. Not everyone jumps at the opportunity of a blind date, though the tendency is tilting, and the blindness inherent to Internet transactions has become culturally attractive, inducing a go-with-the-flow capacity for unguaranteed and fast-paced encounters. Perhaps that is what it takes nowadays, microprocesses and nanoswitches consisting in so many leaps of faith and unavoidable splatters.

The present volume owes its existence to the prescience of Dr. Willis Regier and to the excellent translation of Catherine Porter, whose distinguished work is responsible for bringing a significant number of critical texts to these shores. Anne Dufourmantelle, who has written several outstanding books, including *La sauvagerie maternelle,* one of my favorites, belongs perhaps to the lineage of stellar women writers in France who tend to cover philosophy and psychoanalysis in uncompromising ways, often with relentless integrity. Sarah Kofman, Luce Irigaray, Julia Kristeva, Hélène Cixous, and a few other worthy warriors of critical thought and literary accomplishment make up a historical cluster that has been received with considerable enthusiasm in the Anglo-American reading worlds. I might be tempted to add Derrida to this list, but it's too late to get into a fight about who or what constitutes a "great woman writer," even if made in France, and too late to say why I am constrained by convention to note and tote the gender card. I usually relish such fights (I like to win). Plus, a rumble matches our theme: "Heraclitus conceptualized sexual hunger as combat"(4). Of course, let's just say that, on this occasion, it's not my place to start another fight. Therefore, I surrender my aggressive instinct to the flex and idiomatic rhythms of insight—to the philosophical beat—of Anne Dufourmantelle's singular work.

Translator's Note

Because of differences in citation practices, some material presented in quotation marks in the French original has been converted to paraphrase in the English, and some citations lack source notes. The English translation has been read and approved by Anne Dufourmantelle.

Blind Date . . .
is the term for a meeting between two beings who do not know each other, who may be able to love each other—a meeting organized by someone else who knows them both and who will not be present at the encounter.

Philosophy . . .
begins with astonishment (Aristotle), declares itself the science of being, hopes to provide for the soul, finds its etymology in love of wisdom, imagines spiritual education as its vocation, rights itself into a logic of propositions, lingers in schoolbooks, is written in all languages but is thought to think in just one,
is quietly dying out.

Sex . . .
ends when explanations are required, comments on itself only as it disappears, disrupts any script that seeks to isolate its effects,
is present everywhere, all the time,
is absent everywhere, all the time.

The meeting was scheduled, they say, three thousand years ago. Officially, at least. Since then, it has been continuously postponed.

❧ ❧ ❧ Rendez-vous

From the start, there is astonishment.
And hunger.
To think, to devour.
To be astonished (that the world exists).
To be hungry (for the other).
Aporias, cannibalism, eroticism, stories.

Blind date: an encounter between strangers. Neither protagonist knows the identity of the other. The meeting has been arranged for them. The moment, the occasion, the place will do the rest.

Who imagined the meeting? Who benefits from its staging? What agent is behind this encounter? No one, of course, neither a witness nor a third party who might be questioned, since here only disciplines appear. Sex, philosophy, and their more or less legitimate declensions: metaphysics, the biology of passion, rhetoric, logic, the mechanics of desire, ontology, the chemistry of the attraction between bodies, spiritual exercises, the physics of bodies, the phenomenology of perception, epistemology, *eros, logos* . . . The witness, then, will be impossible to identify; his or her motivation will not be understood. The witness will be said to be time itself, or else it will be said that the organizing principle of the blind date in place for three thousand years is the result of what is nebulously called "technology," at the point where science competes with life to invent intelligence, since no aspect of what fascinates us today is foreign to the *bios,* to the fabrication of life forms.

Sex and philosophy have been deliberately avoiding each other forever, who knows why; perhaps because they are of the same nature? Both seek the realization of an essence, that of desire or that of contemplation; both are treated as dangerous when in use—inflammable, corrupting, and socially subversive. Both are deflected toward multiple ends—consumption, sales, exchanges, power—that they both constantly elude.

And what if sex and philosophy had always interacted by way of blind dates? No need for a friend to arrange a meeting, nor for a witness to watch its unfolding. The event will take place, has taken place, here, now, tomorrow.

❧ ❧ ❧ Preliminaries

How can one philosophize with sex? How can one sexualize philosophy? A blind date is pointless unless it allows the two separate protagonists to linger, with time for each to note the rough spots dotting a terrain on which there are no signposts. Because there is nothing out of the ordinary about the meeting place, it hardly lends itself to clandestine love affairs, nor does it invite solitary contemplation. Neither a Heideggerian Black Forest nor a rugged Nietzschean Sils Maria nor a Socratic banquet hall, it is a landscape open to the horizon, nothing more. With a sky for height and water for movement, the rest is a matter of the moment.

To philosophize about sex is to think of its philosophical preliminaries, its margins, its surroundings, its subterranean periphery, its steep slopes, its white lines. What makes it possible for us to think sex? What is required a priori? How does sex allow itself to be thought? Or rather, no, sex does not allow itself to be thought. One cannot start from two bodies, or several, that give each other orgasmic pleasure, *jouissance*, in order to construct sex as a concept. The image of sex intervenes. A privilege of conceptual installations that rely on forms to "display" sex while keeping its truths out of sight. And in so doing expose it nonetheless. A vast mirror of images, field against field. Pornography, screens, overexposed sex—about which we still understand nothing at all, can say almost nothing at all, because sex is presumed to be a pure event that takes place, nothing more.

How has philosophy conceptualized sex? How has it approached the question a priori? That mingling of bodies, that desire, that hunger? Heraclitus conceptualized combat. Plato, the combat in the soul between the desire for pleasure and the desire for truth. Aristotle, the dynamics of a body moved by passion. Lucretius, the atomization of bodies.

Plotinus, lost unity. Epicurus, dependence on pleasure. The cynics liked to be provocative. Augustine conceptualized the path leading out of the sexual wilderness; Giordano Bruno did the same. Nietzsche sought to demystify the power of reason over the body; Schopenhauer was the first to conceptualize the destiny of the drives. All of them forged a morality; none of them spoke about their own sexual lives. But what philosophy has carefully avoided conceptualizing is what could confound it, namely, desire, inasmuch as desire governs thought and sex alike. Not until the dawn of the eighteenth century did philosophy conceptualize itself as an act or an event outside the sphere of contemplation. It expended too much energy trying to compete with science for the right to produce objective knowledge of the world, trying to comprehend the laws that govern the world, trying to determine what animates the human soul, how the soul moves the body, what makes any body move, how evil can exist and be understood, how death already dwells in life from the start, and how the mind, alone, in exile, never stops contemplating these matters.

❧ ❧ ❧   Two or Three Things We Know about Them . . .

One day, it begins . . . And one suddenly wonders why philosophy never speaks of sex and yet speaks of nothing else. Why don't we think about sex when we read Plato, Kant, Heidegger, Pascal, Malebranche, Avicenna? Why should sex have to remain ignorant of philosophy, which in Greek, as everyone knows, means "love of wisdom," since nothing to do with love is foreign to sex? What is this sort of universal obsession—sex—that is supposed to disappear when we approach the forbidding walls of philosophical discourse? Into what other thing is it supposed to be converted: into pure love of thought? How and why could it be nowhere, or almost, in philosophical language? He who has thought the most deeply loves the most spiritedly, Hölderlin tells us. For obsessions are peculiar in that they can change, can even change their object, but they cannot disappear, precisely because they are conflated with the subject. You obsess me to the extent that I become "you," I incorporate you, I believe you to be closer to me than I am to myself. If sex is an obsession—a quality that it shares, in a way, with philosophy—this is so in that it does not let go of us, ever. Even when we are not thinking about it, not engaging in it, even when we are sleeping, praying, laughing. Sex is the subterranean fiction that makes us beings pledged to "the other," without fail. Philosophy, for its part, is a derivative, secondary obsession. Because philosophy requires that the world be a source of astonishment for us, a source of anxiety and pardon. Thus that there be otherness.

To wonder, yes, why sex runs through everything, including the most resistant concepts, those that form the armature of metaphysics, like so many little metallic ribs: Time, Truth, Measure, Politics, Appetite, Being, Infinity, Face, Causality, Monad . . . All these are foreign to the question of sex, but none emerges unaffected from a confrontation with desire. Sex corrodes everything, including the abstract words that define the attributes of substance, mathematical figures, complex syllogisms. And yet . . . Because we read a philosophical text while forgetting ourselves as subjects of desire, sex must never be mentioned in it. Because we read the pages of a Socratic dialogue the way one ventures off into the distance toward an unknown territory that has been wiped clean of all the old landmarks, we prefer to forget that one enters into words with one's body. Because we read a treatise on logic the way we would climb a wall barehanded, we expect from the hitherto obscure text a sudden revelation—reading as cannibalism, Nietzsche used to say, or thought as the art of eating raw meat—and the memory of a lasting astonishment. The wise man will reach greater depths by struggling to understand the paradox as such and will not try to explain the paradox by understanding that it does not exist, Kierkegaard suggests ironically. And what if the paradox proposed by the philosophic life were precisely this: that underneath it all there is nothing to think but the body? The body as origin and space of thought, the body that imagines and loves, the body that lives and dies, the body that hopes and desires?

But nothing to do with sex . . . neither voluptuousness nor eroticism nor whispering. No mixtures, few affects. The entrance into metaphysics is an exercise in self-surpassment, an effort to breathe with very little oxygen, in which the rigors of syllogisms tussle over a territory lacking emotions, lacking bodies. The philosophic reading takes place outside of "oneself," as if we had no personal involvement, as if neither time nor hunger could affect us. We quickly adopt, with Kant, the progressive path of a reason ennobled by critical consciousness, and we stop to rest a little farther on, before starting the chapter on morality. Or else we venture along the more dangerous roads of Husserlian phenomenology, snow-covered in all seasons, to the point where the landscape completely disappears, and along with it our capacity to judge. Sex will never come up. Not once. Friendship, yes, even love, missteps, lies. Sex is the silent other of philosophy—which had nevertheless taken its task to be that of conceptualizing all being, leaving nothing out, at least long ago, when metaphysics still thought it belonged to the world and thought it was nudging that same world in the direction of clarity.

So, read a few pages at random. Take *Phaedrus,* or Book VII of *The Republic,* the *Nicomachean Ethics,* Augustine's *Confessions,* Descartes's *Discourse on Method,* Pascal's *Pensées,* Hobbes's *Leviathan,* Spinoza's *Ethics,* Nietzsche's *Genealogy of Morals,* Heidegger's *Being and Time,* Kierkegaard's *Fear and Trembling,* Lévinas's *Totality and Infinity,* Derrida's *Specters of Marx* . . . and taste them on an empty stomach. They will provide arms for revolt, dreaming, friendship and pardon, thinking origins and history, believing and refusing to believe. But no eroticism, except perhaps as a metaphor for lost unity.

And yet sex is there, wherever there is astonishment. And hunger.

❧ ❧ ❧ Display

Blind date. A meeting to which the participants go blindly, then. Not really under cover, no. But without knowing . . . who will be there. Who the other will be. And in the expectation of a true encounter. Since one spends one's life waiting for just that, an encounter; and fearing it, too.

Speaking, telling, explaining, commenting, showing, selling, selling oneself. Sex needs to show that it isn't lagging behind, that it, too, can display itself on the mesh of the Net to ensure the cadence, while philosophy exposes itself on public thoroughfares, vituperating through the mouths of authorized thinkers in every medium, however local. An immense gray mush in which a few indigestible morsels of thought still float, weighing on our contemporaries' stomachs. But to list the ways in which thinking is blocked is not yet to say anything at all, for the requirements of solitude and skill posited by thought have not changed in two thousand years, and the quest that opens up our hunger and our astonishment is always the same.

Because it responds first of all to hunger, to the spiritual hunger we call astonishment, philosophy will never exhaust its object. And it is because this hunger lacks a response to the question of evil, to the questions of origins, innocence, and finality, that it incites us to conceptualize beings and the world in an always derivative, secondary manner. This hunger moves along an unknown horizon constituted by the limits of language and the limits of its own ability to interrogate language—limits that are immeasurably difficult to pin down, as the English logicians did not fail to perceive. Indeed, from Husserl and Wittgenstein on, the world in question is a world that physics proposes to describe and whose articulations are provided by logic. "The world is all that is . . . ," Wittgenstein writes; "the facts in logical space are the world. The world divides into facts. Each item can be the case or not the case while everything else remains the same. We picture facts to ourselves."[1] In short, logic as architecture of the world. And he adds, in the *Tractatus:* "in fact all the propositions of logic say the same thing, to wit nothing."[2] If philosophy is a theory of knowledge, a theory of knowledge is always a critique of language. To critique language, however, is to work in thrall to the idea that man can never go beyond a metaphoric description of the world: neither everyday language nor philosophical language will suffice. Whereas the nominalists had tried to show that words correspond exactly to sensations and thus constitute the only solid foundation for knowledge (a concept from which all of psychoanalysis is secretly derived), Mauthner, Wittgenstein, and the school of thought that developed around the turn of the last century in Vienna and then in Cambridge, with Russell, went further, affirming that concepts are at best metaphors for what is perceived by the senses. In any case, they have no "ontological" thickness, and they function like little bolts holding down the articulations of our value judgments; in reality, their impact is purely grammatical.

> "How do you know I'm mad?" said Alice.
> "You must be," said the Cat, "or you wouldn't have come here."
> Alice didn't think that proved it at all; however, she went on:
> "And how do you know that you're mad?"
> "To begin with," said the Cat, "a dog's not mad. You grant that?"

"I suppose so," said Alice.

"Well, then," the Cat went on, "you see a dog growls when it's angry, and wags its tail when it's pleased. Now *I* growl when I'm pleased, and wag my tail when I'm angry. Therefore I'm mad."

"*I* call it purring, not growling," said Alice.

"Call it what you like," said the Cat.[3]

There is no salvation, then, outside of language. In this sense, philosophy "touches" us: it is like a sound, a resonance and a resistance of the world in language, within language.

❧ ❧ ❧ Touching

Philosophy is an art of touching, just as sex is an art of intelligence. Touch is the living experience of the world on the part of what "thinks thought" in us. Philosophy is an art of touching because it experiences what it thinks, because it appears only in and through that act, while sex, for its part, allows us to experience just what is untouchable in the other. That other who can be explored, restrained, enveloped, consoled, hurt, and brought to jouissance unveils in the rawest and most exposed intimacy the fact that some part will always escape not only desire but also even sex (a word that refers both to the sex act and to the associated organs), and that there is something untouchable in the body itself. Spinoza's genius lay here: transcendence is in the most intimate proximity to the self, and you don't know it. No one knows what a body can do.[4] The body—its exact resonance, its matter, its history—is located in the blank spot of desire, of speech, of thought.

Sex is not named by philosophy. Or only in such an impoverished, caricatural manner that it's almost funny: appetites, affections, lasciviousness—sex is found lying in ambush in a blank spot, in a deafening silence. Everywhere except where love is in question. Ignored, demonized, effaced, sex is the first philosophical aporia, the locus of philosophy's obscure, nocturnal, indiscernible astonishment. Sex is touch unable to express itself; philosophy, which has no tactile surface, no skin or nerve endings, is an art of touching concepts: their imbrications, their meticulous constructions, their silence. A touch other than that of the skin, comparable to a musician's touch, that is, a touch that sets up a precise virtuosic resonance in which the world is engaged.

Sex experiences itself as a philosophical aporia, a body mingling with another body or with other plural bodies, a world mingling with another world, another skin, another voice, and one that comes undone just where it is resolved. To enter into jouissance is to be nevertheless at that place where the body no longer belongs to the body, where it becomes pure resonance, pure intelligence of the other, and, in that abandonment, "thought."

❦ ❦ ❦ Excuses

Were sex and philosophy supposed to meet . . . since there has always been secret commerce between them? In mutual ignorance of their attachments, to be sure. Why this blind date? Which one will surprise the other? Which will seduce the other, and how? What secret will be revealed? The alibis evoked in order to avoid the meeting were effective for a long time. The lives of the philosophers offer very little insight on the subject. Obsessed by sex as much as any of us, the philosophers nevertheless wrote nothing at all about the hidden side of their textual asceticism. For sex and philosophy have in common at least the fact that they are obsessions. There is no true thought that is not obsessional, that does not turn endlessly around the same question, that does not return again and again to the modalities of an unformulated question. An obsession that operates in the shade, shaping every life, every thought, every work, because what is ultimately at stake is the same desire. Sex, love, philosophy.

If philosophy is obsessional, this is because its object is forgotten. Philosophy does not know what it is looking for. It is etymologically devoted to the love of wisdom, and that is all. That is a great deal. Philosophy is obsessed with a traversal that no shore will assuage, no work will achieve. The light promised to the prisoners of the Cave will dazzle those who free themselves from their chains to reach it. They will go back to contemplate the film projected on the wall in the guise of reality, because illusion is a stronger passion than truth. So when the time comes to live out, day after day, what philosophy had sought in the ideal, they will protect their naked eyes from the blinding glare of the sun in a sheltered space, the umbilical space of dreams. The violence of truth does not tolerate shade. A single obsession guides sex and philosophy, *eros* and *logos*, the obsession with an absolute seeing that would not be the visible and that would not kill.

❧ ❧ ❧   Little Arrangements among Friends

Sex and philosophy: not the arranged, always missed meeting of mind and body that has darkened more pages in twenty centuries than all biblical commentary put together. Sex is an act; so is philosophy. Acts that incite humanity to love and to be free. And this is indeed what makes them dangerous, since they do not leave the one who uses them unaffected. Sex and philosophy are exercises in living, in the Stoics' sense: to approach them is already to experience them. To alienate oneself in them (take the risk), to involve oneself in them (not always), to give up (often). Sex is said to be action, not thought. Philosophy, too: it never stops thinking itself. Sex and philosophy are humanity's two major passions; and perhaps precisely for this reason they have been kept secret, *sostenuto,* in affinity with the minor modes of pain, passion, and intimacy. We are afraid of everything that confirms the acknowledgment of our dependency, afraid, that is, of sex, love, and thought—which probably amount to the same thing. We should like to see ourselves as free, as masters of ourselves, at least to some degree. Yet sex and philosophy alike are rigorous and fatal experiments in chemistry. With a remainder of silence around them that words surround in all directions.

The lives of the philosophers hint at the domination of sex, but here, shhh, there is nothing to be said . . . Foucault's back-room encounters in New York, Deleuze's sexual ambiguities, Kant's strange asceticism, Kierkegaard's lesson in seduction, Nietzsche's divagations, Pascal's challenges, Descartes's secrets, and Abelard's, and Augustine's, Socrates' temptations, the Cynics' and the Stoics' freedom? . . . No, nothing will be said about the way desire may have haunted these philosophers. It is owing to the intelligence that sex reveals—and not, as is supposed, owing to its stupidity, there is nothing less stupid than sex—that we can guess why so much effort has been expended to fight it, to make it guilt-ridden, to bury it in shame, to deny the freedom that bears it and that also constitutes its power of revolt: so that the enigma of desire can be reduced to the expression of a mechanical need. Because for a long time sex has aroused hatred. We know this; we see the effects of the phenomenon every day: rape and the obscenity of traffic in bodies through ever more ungraspable networks are only among its latest avatars. Sex shares this battle with philosophy, an object of hatred par excellence, as the death of Socrates attests. And we have yet to conceptualize the threats they both pose to the human community, threats that make sex and philosophy the objects of so many rules and taboos, so much violence. Hatred of thought and hatred of the desiring body have many lands, many exiles, and many foliations in common.

❧ ❧ ❧   Here One Does Not Learn

The taboo on thinking and the taboo on loving may lie at the foundation of the social body, in an obscure way, because the freedom that thinking and loving arouse emboldens people to act against oppression, against the dictatorship of stupidity, against cowardly behavior, false appearances, and self-evident truths. Sex and philosophy share a desire to taste a truth that no one can have predigested for them, whether it be corporeal or conceptual; this truth is the object of their doubt and their questioning, of patient exploration and not of any teaching, however brilliant. Neither sex nor philosophy can be taught. At most, one may acquire the rules of reasoning, the principles for linking logical propositions, the history of concepts in history, just as one may ply one's body to the demands of certain figures. "Compel a person to an opinion, a conviction, a belief—in all eternity, that I cannot do," says Kierkegaard. "But one thing I can do, in one sense the first thing (since it is the condition for the next thing: to accept this view, conviction, belief), in another sense the last thing if he refuses the next: I can compel him to become aware."[5] But to become aware is already to be available to the other. With the other, in a special proximity of mind, body, words, presence. Awareness opens the way of that presence to self and to the other, long before there is consent.

Because finally, in hatred of sex, in hatred of the invention and construction of concepts, we always find, again and again, a trace of terror at the upheaval produced by an encounter. An encounter with the other—the conceptualized and caressed other, the carnal and spiritual other—that definitively upsets anyone who keeps the appointment. No one is exempt from having one day truly risked his or her thought along the pathways of philosophy, that is, of the love of wisdom, just as no one is exempt from committing himself or herself to the sexual love of another being, which means that s/he is one and several, that s/he has a body and that s/he is a body, and that the world comes to a sudden halt at the place of this skin, this hair, this name; it means that everything is begun and resolved there in the moment of the encounter, which stretches the boundaries of the possible to infinity in order to test its density, the degree to which it is alive.

❧ ❧ ❧ Gravity of Sex, Lightness of Philosophy

The same force drives a man or a woman to love and to think. No doubt because sex is a grave thing whereas philosophy is light in its essence, jubilatory and musical. Sex and philosophy have never stopped interchanging their gravity. The latter bears the weight of forgetfulness of being, the better to forget that irony is consuming its horizon, time wrested away from death, thought cornered by the certainty of its own disappearance, in the imminent erasure of all traces. That is to say, of our own death, everyone's. The certainty that we are only passing through, neither more nor less than bit players, a time, a space, a name. Philosophy cannot be grave; it no longer has the means to be grave if it wants to think presence, the pure present, the decisive instant, it must finally enter into lightness. Such was the Nietzschean diagnosis. Nietzsche preferred Verdi to Wagner, signifying the extent to which the spirit of weightiness was doing philosophy an injustice. Irony and jubilation have long been viewed as obstacles to the spirit of seriousness that was supposed to ground metaphysics in its titanic work of restoring being. Until certain thinkers introduced a breach into the structure. Jubilation, joy—this was also Spinoza's favorite theme. Joy as the essence of being. But philosophical lightness was also to be the incomparable lucidity of Wittgenstein, who preferred a prosaic interrogation of the meaning of our grammatical propositions to the rhetorical apparatus of "big metaphysics."

Gravity devolved, perhaps, to sex alone . . . First because we owe it our lives (while we wait for cloning, our survival still depends on sex), and then because we owe it nothing, actually. A space of pure exchange that we would like to bind to all possible constraints. When in fact it obeys only the complex machinery of desire.

Sex cares nothing for philosophy. It is assigned to the body alone, to its subtle mechanics, its unpredictable humors, its fluids, its breath, its density. Sex is accountable to the body alone. At least this is the way we imagine it. And this is just as foolish as to say that thought is not of the body, since it is nothing but that, of the body. Sex needs intelligence; it weighs on every human life with the weight of its absence, of its generation, of the taboos to which we have subjected it. Sex is nourished by the intelligence of desire, by the appropriation and the blocking of desire, by its filters, by the lies in which desire is clothed, the oaths that it betrays, the repetitions that it carries out through the figure of its multiple orchestrations.

❧ ❧ ❧ Body Moor Flesh Landscape Memory

Sex is not the body. It is even the forgetting of the body. It is what makes us, in jouissance, feel desire, or sadness, excitement, fear, longing— everything about the body that is not "the body," that is, flesh. When the body becomes world, landscape, moor, sand, language, collage, collapse, memory, the entire body is convoked as *other* than flesh. Other, indeed, for it is a matter of otherness, for philosophy as well as for sex. Their history is the same, like two sides of a single coin stamped with the seal of that recognition.

At the very outset, philosophy and sex have to do with the Other, *l'Autre* with a capital *A,* as Lacan would say—which is not to say all that much, however. That there is otherness, yes, this is strange. Both sex and philosophy vouch for this strangeness. For the very fact that there is otherness, that is, world. And the impossibility of embracing it all. Effraction, cloaking. The other, that is, you. I can eat you, fuck you, leave you, caress you, understand you, possess you, abandon you, conceptualize you, compel you, analyze you. Nothing suffices. There is this initial shock, which lies at the beginning of philosophy, like an equation without remainder and nevertheless unresolved.

Why is there something rather than nothing? Why, and how, do you exist? Since "I" come from "you" . . . Since we are born of another, and we die alone. Philosophy tries to explain itself with a particular test that consists in making astonishment a language for deciphering the world. Philosophy is a language for coming to terms with the foreign body that I call "you," the plural world that persists in being other than itself, the language that makes us beings of words and desire. Philosophy was thus a metapsychology long before the invention of psychoanalysis. Freud did not invent that journey; he followed in the footsteps of Socrates, Epictetus, Augustine, Duns Scotus, Maimonides, Spinoza, Kant. To be sure, Freud, Ferenczi, Jung, and some others ripped the mask away from hysterical madness by revealing that this madness hid a quite rational logic of desire, a logic that subjugates us all insofar as we prefer to know nothing about it. But the philosophers were the first to sound the depths of the human soul by not taking literally, as it were, the mystifications with which, through words, it likes to surround itself. This violent therapy has an inventor: Socrates. It was with words and against them that he sought out the dwelling place of truth. A different truth from the one to which we are pinned down by the illusions of meaning and consciousness, that is, of belief—in short, the entire panoply used by the ego to shore up its power. A modest truth that specifically does not wish to let itself be abused by the deceptive power of discourse. A power that holds us in its sway. And increasingly, since we sacrifice almost everything to words, to language. Using the power of elucidation, of analysis, that is language (language that contains, engrammatically, the very figure of our desire) to disalienate ourselves from it, to glimpse something other through the mesh, is a true philosophical task. It presupposes something like a musical or mathematical harmony, the reflection of a cosmological world, the Greeks thought, in which everything would be in its place: gods, heavens, polities, men, images—each reflecting the constellations of the other, their subtle mechanisms, their finely chiseled precision. Today we no longer advance in an ordered world: no more celestial hierarchy, no more mathematics of the spheres or faithful polities; the fact remains that truth is still waiting to be thought. For philosophy is of an extreme precision; it advances whispering and with measured steps, against our predilection for chimerical constructions.

Sex is not bodies, as philosophy is not concepts; each is an act, a relation, and a language.

❧ ❧ ❧ On the Illusion of Being Immortal

We prefer illusion to all else—this was Schopenhauer's diagnosis, well before Freud—because this dispenses us from thinking that we are mortal. But one does not flush out the power of that decoy without danger. Because all this will end one day . . . In three or four generations at most, no trace will remain of our moods, our convulsions, our rebellions. Except for what has crossed over, what has germinated, what has been inscribed even without the revelation of any legacy. Without a clear vision of what any of this is worth . . . Thus through family secrets and other shadowy genealogical regions, we can watch first names come in cycles, the strange repetition of dates of birth, engagement, or death, the same names of villages, countries, and frontiers at fifty years' remove, the same wounds of body or soul . . . a whole treasure trove of meaning is perpetuated from generation to generation, even though human beings rarely seek to decipher it. This transmission remains unknown to us because it frightens us.

Our finite nature is a prop for both sex and philosophy. Sex responds to death by canceling out time; so does philosophy. The one uses desire, and so does the other. But sex suspends time for as long as the conjunction of bodies lasts, for as long as we are obsessed by desire for a skin, a face, a name, as long as we remain caught up in the sway of the moment and the act. Jouissance can be construed as a moment provisionally outside of time and without duration, in Bergson's sense, a space of pure letting-go on the subject's part, in which forgetting time prefigures forgetting death, forgetting the mortal body. A blackout via the senses, a flash without a future.

Philosophy, for its part, proceeds by stages. It posits an argument, reasons, sidesteps the issue, delivers a judgment, calls it into question, takes one more step in the direction of the logic of being, and in the process (even when its object is time itself, for time is after all one of its favorite subjects) it sweeps time under the rug, believes it is escaping death by conceptualizing death. An old magician's trick. Philosophy acts as if, by conceptualizing time and by conceptualizing human beings who conceptualize the world, it can go back to the initial point at which thought escapes time. Thought that would receive thought as not subject to the alteration of time. An old ruse, yes, but an effective one. Concepts do not die or age, they change with time by virtue of being manipulated. But what can philosophy do about that? Philosophy uses concepts as if they were so many magic little rungs from which a timeless ladder could be constructed. And to reach what? Celestial truths? No, desire. In *Twilight of the Idols,* Nietzsche writes: "All the higher culture and literature . . . grew up on the soil of sexual interests. You can search everywhere in it for gallantry, the senses, sexual competition, 'woman'—and you will never search in vain."[6]

One will never search in vain because these are the umbilical cord of dreams, the melting pot of all alchemy, that which in the blank spaces of language designates desire as the center of gravity of all activity of thought, secret or exposed. Only time erodes concepts; it unveils the changing, volatile essence of the desire that moves them. And thus reveals the erratic character of all truth.

Why, then, believe that one could exempt thought from time, from mortal becoming, any more than jouissance? What is the savage soul of desire that would guarantee almost by magic the tranquil assurance of its traversal of the ages and the centuries? Nowhere do we find a forgetting of death, but philosophy, like sex, will have lived a long time with the illusion that it entertains an ultimately privileged and serene relation with eternity. And it is hard to intervene and disturb that understanding, as it is hard to wake a sleeping child. The idea that thought has the privilege of establishing itself in a kingdom from which all effractions of time are banished is equaled only, perhaps, by the obscure certainty of two persons who are making love that they have, at that instant, no more accounts to render to time.

❧ ❧ ❧ Some Alibis for a Nonencounter

A blind date is hard to avoid, once one has accepted the principle of leaving the arrangements to a well-meaning friend or a neutral third party (agencies that give you seven minutes to find a kindred spirit, seven minutes, really . . . isn't love at first sight instantaneous?). However, if the identity of the other party is suspected, one can attempt *in extremis* to avoid committing oneself to the adventure by falling back on some alibis.

As far as sex is concerned, the suspicion was well founded . . . and philosophy could with good reason take the meeting to be a trap. As a primary discourse (that is, a discourse on first things), philosophy constituted itself, in Greece, in opposition to the universe of tragedy, pathos, and myth. Against the tyranny of belief, against the order of fallacious political discourses, against the school of rhetoric, against the illusion of the senses and of passion, against approximation of judgments of taste and opinion, against likelihood and likeness. And one of the common denominators we find in everything that philosophy opposes is emotion. Philosophy is intent on strengthening us against emotion; thus it makes rules designed to discern what *compromises* us in emotion. Driving out this enemy that has set up camp within the walls, that is, within the self, is a saving task for philosophic exigency. Emotion is to be proscribed twice over, first because it alters reason and leads us to the side of the *doxa*—imaginary, sentimental foolishness—and then because it taints all logic with a dose of indelible pathos; in short, emotion is the element of impurity that corrodes thought in its infinitesimal progression toward the truth of essences. Philosophy, in this sense, would be the realm of the separate, the unmixed, the realm of naked truth. A tireless center for sorting and testing. And not only since Descartes, for reason has always been understood as having to protect itself from contamination by the senses. To succeed in conceptualizing "the idea," one has to gain access to its purity.

But we must be careful not to be too quick to confine the origin of philosophical discourse to the conflict between reason and emotion, *logos* and *mythos*. For the task of philosophy also lies in the Python's answer to Socrates, "*Gnoti seauton*": know thyself. Here we reencounter the "take care of yourself" motif that traversed all of Greece through the time of the Neoplatonists and beyond, up to the early Christians. But the "self" in question is precisely what all human beings have in common. For what is the meaning of "caring for oneself" or "taking care of oneself" in Plato's dialogues? Socrates puts it this way: you who are concerned about the world, about appearances, about politics, you must be concerned first of all about yourself. Turn toward that self with which you must be concerned; know yourself. Know who you are. To discover this "self" of which Socrates speaks, Plato's text uses the metaphor of the eye. If the soul is like the eye of knowledge (French *connaissance*), we must ask under what conditions and in what way an eye can see itself. A mirror is not the only reflecting surface for an eye that seeks to look at itself. When someone's eye looks into another eye that is like itself, it sees itself. Thus an identity in nature is the condition under which an individual can know what s/he is. But it is especially in the pupil that the eye sees itself, that is, at the site where the principle of vision is realized. The eye does not see itself in the eye; the eye sees itself in the principle of vision. What happens if this comparison is applied to the soul? It tells us that the soul will see itself only by directing its gaze toward an element of the same nature as itself, and more precisely by applying its gaze to the very principle that constitutes the nature of the soul, namely, thought and knowledge (French *savoir*, Greek *to phronein, to eidenai*). What is this element that undergirds thought and knowledge? It is the divine element. Thus the soul can know itself by turning toward the divine. Responding to Alcibiades, who is questioning him, Socrates refers to the region of a soul in which the virtue of soul—wisdom—is situated, and he goes on to say that "this part of [the soul] resembles God, and whosoever looks at this, and comes to know all that is divine, will gain thereby the best knowledge of himself."[7] As soon as it is in contact with the divine, then, the soul will be endowed with wisdom (*sophrosune*). Only at that moment will the soul be able to distinguish what is true from what is false. It will be able to conduct itself justly and it will be able to govern. For Platonism, access to truth requires a spiritual movement on the part of a soul that has a relation to itself and to the divine: to the divine because it has a relation to itself, to itself because it has a relation to the divine. For nothing can be elevated to the power of the idea but the idea itself. In the face of the scandal of a world subjected to the alteration of time and to the duplicity of appearances, the mathematical harmonies are convoked to attest to the fact that the human spirit can succeed in conceiving unalterable truths. But human passions intervene, disrupting discernment and preventing the subject from coinciding absolutely with his or her soul. Such is the composite of body and soul that has to be raised up to contemplation of the Idea. Nothing personal is worthy of being an object of science. There can be no slippage from one subject to another, from one utterance to another: the philosopher's task is to compartmentalize, discern, separate. The culmination of the Platonic work will preside over this separation for a long time. Until Descartes, then, to think is to elevate oneself to that which is of the same nature as the soul; it is to achieve unity of being. Thus all spiritual education is, par excellence, a philosophical trajectory from the realm of vague shadows to the pure brilliance of the good. It is an asceticism of unequaled rigor that requires us to renounce passion and indeed to renounce whatever carries us away, in short, whatever mixes thought with something other than itself, namely, emotion. Emotion is the mixture, so corrosive to the soul, of desire and idea, the glimpsed brilliance of the good and the voluptuous sensation that the good can also be attained with the body, and in life.

❧ ❧ ❧ Alterations

Sex, for its part, likes nothing so much as mixtures. Mixtures of skins, salivas, humors, organs, words to the point of delirium, images, as well: sex makes do with anything, can put everything to use. And yet sex has found itself using the same alibi as philosophy, namely an instinctive suspicion of any form of emotion. You have been imbued with this idea from the cradle, you will recognize it easily: sex is not love, sex is not emotion, sex is nothing but sex, a pure quest for pleasure that culminates in orgasm and reduces everything else to oblivion. Sex is not love; it needs rawness, sensation, nothing more; emotion almost distorts jouissance, tugging it in the direction of love of the other, toward loss, abandonment, renunciation. Emotion intrudes to disrupt the figures of jouissance by mixing in something other than sex.

This mistrust of emotion is a heavy legacy, a very old constraint: even today, it is risky to challenge it, to dare to say "but wait, sex *is* love, it does not preclude emotion, it is nourished by emotion just as philosophy is." There is no real thought without emotion—no sex, either. Emotion is the signature of alterity. It is a sign, precisely, that there is otherness, and that the other in question is reaching us. Aesthetic emotion, for example, survives only if the landscape enters you, becomes another skin, a momentary substitute for your own. And for this to happen, a certain awareness of the world has to have come about. Emotion is an affliction overcome, an immense sorrow that one has barely surmounted, just enough not to be swallowed up by it; sometimes it approaches the sublime, but it constantly reverts to sorrow, to the primal, existential sorrow of being "separated." Emotion is absolutely involuntary. It is a pure inner event; it happens, that is all; it surprises you, it disarms you, it insists and upsets the order of thoughts—as it does every other order, moreover.

Under the sway of emotion, you are another: even your memory, even your capacity for distancing yourself are affected. You act under the constraint of a force that comes for its part without constraint, along the path of desire. Emotion is a cursor indicating that something has taken place, something is in the process of taking place here and now, and one can do nothing about it. To repress emotion is to set in motion a whole mechanism of censorship and avoidance that may well succeed in deceiving you for a while—in other words, your emotion may be temporarily suppressed—but sooner or later it will exact its revenge by unfolding with much more violence, having breached all the inner dikes to the point where you can no longer find any trace of the first act that had given it support. Emotion is pure event. It relies on what we do not know about ourselves when the world approaches. When the world arrives, when it breaks the skin, breaks through the fragile abstraction that we are in order to make us experience the pain of being separated. Separated from what is. Light, wind, sand, astonishment, daylight, you. Emotion makes us think. But philosophy hates emotion. Has it come to hate what makes us think? This is a strange loop, in perpetual motion. Pendular. Emotion feeds thought, which in return represses it. Thought advances constrained by the world, but it seeks to forget that it comes from the world. Hence this slow, perpetual, frenzied combat of philosophy against the world. No, I owe you nothing, my thinking does not start with you or coincide with you, I function alone in the enchanted circle of pure idealities. Contemplation is my only passion, says the philosopher. I observe and I discern what lies beneath the deceptive movement of appearances, in the peregrinations of ideas, over and beyond our overwhelmed senses. Here is the culmination of metaphysics, the aptly named discipline that rises above the world to think the world and to think against it, to think being and only being, to think mankind as if no one were there to think that thought, when it transits for a second through a human brain, acquires a sensibility, a voice. In these territories of the mind, deserted by all afflictions, philosophy would be impersonal. And yet thought is nourished solely by what alters it so profoundly that it has to imagine another heaven, another form, another passage allowing it to cross over and see.

Sex also feeds on emotion, and it, too, would like to forget emotion, abstract itself, behave as if it were only a mechanics of desire organized for all time in perfect adequacy to the use of the body. A use that would be reduced to a few clockwork motions of our fantasies. Sex is an act. But not merely: it is an act caught up in the event that takes place. It can be understood only as an act, but unlike any other act, it cannot be separated from the excitement that animates it. What excitement? The excitement that anticipates pleasure. That presupposes and precedes it, mentally and physically. Of what nature is this anticipation? In a lovely text in *Ideas,* Husserl analyzes the way in which perception is nourished by anticipation (protension) and memory, even when what is perceived happens to us in the moment, since time is antecedent to our capacity to perceive and forms its protective casing, its intimate grammar.

Thus philosophy has used its hatred of emotion to avoid thinking about sex. Or rather to avoid coming to encounter it on the terrain of the mixing of humors. It has withdrawn a priori: no, this is not its realm, it wants to conceptualize only ideality; the entire realm of the visible and the flesh belong to it, but flesh "envisaged," in Paul Ricoeur's phrase, that is, flesh already subtracted from the body, already sublimated, flesh that is all gaze. For in reality philosophy is not frightened by the mechanics of sex, only by its emotional charge, its power to seduce, a power that would undo the workings of philosophical concepts one by one and tilt them gently toward the incomprehensible. And the major interest of this alibi—no emotion—was that sex, as a mirror, could use it, too. Could proscribe emotion with the same forcefulness, the same elegance, the same scorn. But let us make a short detour by way of China. When concepts are articulated there—respiration, emptiness, perfection, whiteness, rhythm—one suddenly glimpses, but with all the difficulty of the untranslatable, what a language has at its disposal when thought approaches bodies and time in this other way, that is, through respiration, through what unifies and connects the empty and the full, when thought is not afraid of what would exclude it, namely, emptiness, but also love. In the face of being, the Orient has conceptualized capacity; in the face of God, regulation; in the face of perception, François Jullien teaches us, it has conceptualized respiration. There is no eroticism that is not a humanism, no philosophy that is not regulation. Nothing is separated, nothing is fractured. We cannot conceive, as the Orient can, of a blind date between philosophy and sex, because it would be a question of the self-same body that loves, thinks, and is delirious, that eroticizes, infinitizes, and questions; it would be the same thought that makes itself skin and the same skin that becomes the loop traced by the brush to rejoin the instant.

❧ ❧ ❧ Varieties of Intemperance

Neither Greek nor Latin offers us a notion comparable to that of "sexuality." As Foucault demonstrates masterfully in his last study, *The Use of Pleasure,* Greek has a whole series of words designating various gestures or acts that we call "sexual," but the overall rubric under which all these gestures, acts, and practices fall is much more difficult to grasp. The Greeks commonly used an eponymous adjective, *ta aphrodisia* (Aphrodisian), which was later rendered in Latin by *venerea,* that is, "things or pleasures of love, sexual relations, bodily acts, voluptuous behaviors . . ." In French, the word *sexuality* did not appear before the nineteenth century, and it does not encompass the multiplicity of meanings designated by the Latin and Greek terms.

In *Laws,* Plato invokes the existence of three major, fundamental appetites that have to do with food, drink, and reproduction, the latter being the strongest. In ancient Greece, sexuality as a dominant appetite, as a passion from which a subject was understood to be alienated, was clearly a pathology of excess, or at least such was its hyperbolic virtuality. Socrates asks his interlocutor in *The Republic* whether he is acquainted with "any pleasure greater or keener than sexual pleasure."[8] If the danger, for a rational being, is that he or she may be carried away by sexual pleasure, this is because sexual passion is capable of superseding all others and affecting the subject's capacity to think, to discern, and to behave as a citizen.

The other essential signifier of Greek thought insofar as human behavior is concerned is the *kairos,* the opportune moment. This is among the most important, and the most delicate, objectives in the art of making use of pleasures. Plato reminds us of this, again in *Laws:* happy is he who knows what must be done when it must be done and the extent to which it must be done. When Plato speaks of the need to control the three major fundamental appetites, he evokes the need for reinforcement by "the Muses and the gods of contests [*theoi agonioi*]."[9] The long tradition of spiritual combat, which would later take on so many diverse forms, was already clearly articulated in classical Greek thought. This tradition also allows us to trace the emergence of an agonistic relation with the self, a battle to be fought and events that take place between self and self. What constituted negativity par excellence for the Greeks was obviously not the fact of loving both sexes or preferring one's own sex to the other; it was being passive with respect to pleasures. Mastering one's pleasures and submitting them to the *logos* amount to one and the same thing: "In the moderate person," Aristotle says, "the appetitive should be in harmony with reason,"[10] and despite all the differences that oppose the Platonic tripartite division of the soul to the Aristotelian conception at the time of the *Nicomachean Ethics,* it is indeed in terms of superiority of reason over appetites that *sophrosune*—wisdom, discernment—is characterized. For Aristotle, "the desire for the pleasant is insatiable and indiscriminate, in a mindless person"; desire will thus increase to an excessive degree if one "is not ready to obey and under the control of the ruling element"; and the ruling element in question is the *logos,* to which the "appetitive" faculty must conform.[11] Finally, in Plato, the exercise of the *logos* in temperance appears in a third form: that of the recognition of the self by the self. Self-knowledge that leads to the practice of virtue and mastery of one's own desires is a Socratic theme par excellence, as is attested by the spiritual struggle in *Phaedrus*.[12] Thus the soul's relation to truth is at once that which establishes *eros* in its movement, strength, and intensity, and that which helps the soul extricate itself from any dependency and allows it to accede to true love of knowledge. The relation to truth, for Plato, is first of all a matter of *measure:* its ontological structure entails regulating excess in order to allow subjects to desire without being obliterated by the disproportion of their desires; this structure ensures the possibility of a political subject and a subject by right. The underlying principle had already been formulated by Heraclitus: "One ought to quench insolence more than a flaring fire."[13]

As for Aristotle, when he names the principle of all things, the immoveable Prime Mover (*to proton kinoun*), he comes very close to what we call desire, namely, a force that mobilizes everything without being moved itself. Jacques Derrida develops the argument:

> Neither moving itself nor being itself moved, the actuality of this pure energy sets everything in motion, a motion of return to self, a circular motion, Aristotle specifies, because the first motion is always cyclical. And what induces or inspires this is a desire. God, the pure actuality of the Prime Mover, is always at once erogenous and thinkable. He is, so to speak, desirable (*erômenon*), the first desirable (*to proton orekton*) as the first intelligible (*to proton noē ton*) thinking itself, as thought thinking itself (*hē noēsis noēseôs noēsis*) (*Metaphysics* 12.1072a–b, 1074b). Aristotle also defines this first principle, and this will be important for us, as a life (*dia-goge:* in his commentary on this passage, Alexander of Aphrodisias uses *zoe* for life and *zen* for living), a kind of life, a way of leading life, comparable to the best of what we might enjoy for a brief time (*mikron kronon*) in our life (*Metaphysics* 12.1072b). It is thus a life that exceeds the life of human beings, a life lived by the Prime Mover in a constant, continuous, and unending fashion, something that is for us impossible (*adunaton*). That is why the *energeia* of this pure activity is "pleasure" (*hedone*), the circular pleasure taken in oneself [*jouissance de soi*].[14]

❧ ❧ ❧ On Sex Kept Secret

Sex has to be kept secret to be tolerated. It may well govern our appetites, but in secret. Now, to philosophize is to remain on the side of
reason, justness, proportion. Sex, for its part, is a matter of need, dependency, affliction. We are drawn to it time after time. Sex is violence,
even when it brings us to jouissance; it is excess par excellence. And
yet we have no choice but to take on the task of entering the darkness
of that violence. Breaching its thickness, its density, its secrecy. For
there is a pact that seals body and word together, a pact without which
human beings fall ill. They become sick with a desire of which they are
unaware, sick with a deadly silence, sick with a madness they believe
is foreign to the soul. "The thought that thinks more than it thinks is
Desire," Blanchot writes. But this desire that belongs to darkness and
to the radical absence of God does not seek to be satisfied. It is the
very place from which thought is born, and yet it exceeds thought.
Blanchot goes on:

> Desire is separation itself become that which attracts: an interval
> become *sensible,* an absence that turns back into presence. Desire
> is this turning back when in the depth of night, when everything
> has disappeared, disappearance becomes the density of the shadow
> that makes flesh more present, and makes this presence more heavy
> and more strange, without name and without form; a presence one
> cannot then call either living or dead, but out of which everything
> equivocal about desire draws its truth.[15]

That desire lies on the side of the void, or at least very close by. Because
in the manner of the God of Eckhart and the Kabbalists, the god of the
Tsimstum when he withdraws from creation, it is nothingness that is
at the origin of all creation, a mystery that begins with retraction, lack,
sacrifice, God's consent to exile himself from everything. Such a desire
is the motion of life originating in a radical lack, an appeal to respond
originating in silence, an act of existence that begins in a place where
there is only absence.

Philosophy has been a religious matter for a long time. And God
was not in bodies . . . Or if so, then dangerously. It is as if the question
of the Incarnation had inflicted an open wound on the thought that

came from Greek and Latin history, a body of thought in which the body was glorious before it was suspected of being shameful. In this sense, Christ brought the body and flesh back into the heart of philosophical thought, from which the body had been exiled at least for a time. And from Augustine to Hegel, metaphysics found itself charged with the crushing responsibility of justifying the existence of a mortal God, mortal like any human.

Around the fourth century C.E., when Constantine converted to Christianity, the structure of the Catholic corpus was established, in particular with the rejection of heresies. St. Augustine occupies an inaugural position in this post-Pauline "second Christianity," in which flesh and the body gradually took on a negative value that later extended to everything that had anything at all to do with desire. If what was condemned in the Hellenic world was excess in all its forms, and not the appetites of the flesh as such, the ideal of wisdom as measured desire and the pathway toward the good underwent an absolute change of value with the advent of Christianity. The idea of original sin, formulated essentially by Paul and Augustine, was applied to all humanity; human beings were charged with an ineradicable debt, a responsibility for evil and sin from which nothing could relieve them. During Christianity's first ten centuries, every possibility for spiritualizing *eros* collapsed, except in the figures of monastic renunciation or sainthood. Only with courtly love do we see resurgent codes governing spiritualized combat and amorous encounters in which the "joye" of love is associated with a spiritual quest. But "joye" is also ravishment, rapture. In the medieval period, ravishment came about only through rape. And a hero did not allow himself to rape. He could dwell in his lady's love at a price: ravishment transformed into song, poetry, and memory.

The Christian denial of the body is not disdain for the body, not even a *rejection* of the body; it is the awareness that nothing can save us from the human condition. That being born of flesh afflicts us with an original debt to evil, abandonment, pain, betrayal, for which we all have to answer. Each one of us, in other words, inasmuch as each one of us is a human being, a being delivered over to humanity, is affected by the question of evil or original sin prior to any act, any speech, any intention. In this respect, a child is no more free of sin than a pious adult who renounces all attachments. Baptism opens up an abyss, as it were, as far as the innocence of children is concerned. If an unbaptized infant cannot be buried in a Christian cemetery, this is because all human innocence is secondary, always supplemental, imparted as a sacrament by a human community. Thus this innocence signifies what separates it from any "naturalness" of good. The question of innocence will bring the West to consider childhood as an antechamber leading to the age of reason, a period of latency in which it is almost already too late to be saved and still too early to understand. Children will thus belong to whoever is willing to train them, because there is in them—there is in us—neither wisdom nor love that could save us, in advance, simply by virtue of our being human, from anything at all.

❧ ❧ ❧ Shame and the Question of Innocence

Sex is associated with shame. The indelible shame that displays itself just as much as it keeps silent. Sex expresses this shame on the part of the subject: shame at being in the grip of desire, shame at being unable to exhaust desire. But the shame to which the subject is subjected cannot simply be explained away by religious education or even by the morality produced by twenty centuries of Christianity. This shame is broader, deeper, more secret. It has ramifications that plunge into the very heart of the constitution of the psyche. For sexuality, when it bursts forth in childhood, is always overly violent. Intrusive, chaotic, incomprehensible, it appears in the child's eyes as an inexplicable and troubling struggle whose stakes remain hidden.

Childhood is foreign to philosophy. In the West, philosophers have granted childhood neither status nor interest nor consideration of any sort, apart from a few treatises on morality and spiritual edification. Childhood has been viewed as an age devoid of questioning and moral choice. At best, the childhood of humanity has been reflected as a golden age without war or affections. If philosophy has thus neglected childhood, sex, for its part, has maintained a relation with childhood that is called "perverse" today. To imagine a child thrust into the "play" of sex is precisely to imagine a child wrenched away from childhood; it is to instrumentalize children for the purpose of a sexual pleasure about which we have preferred to think that children understand nothing. It is to desire jouissance in the annihilation of the other, in the abject act of putting an end to innocence. Except that perversion is a recent concept, as is the protection of childhood.

Shame raises the question of transgressions and taboos. What has established the need to posit a moral prohibition? Is it transgression that has called for the taboo on murder and incest, or is it on the basis of the reality of evil that the moral prohibition as we know it in the West has been constructed? If evil came first, how could it be apprehended as such from the standpoint of a prohibition that did not yet exist? These questions, among others, caused a lot of ink to flow from the pens of eighteenth-century encyclopedists and moralists. Sexuality, to the extent that it signified excess, the nonhumanized, brought back into view, in the characteristics of animals, that which escapes all sociality. Animality has thus become, par excellence, that which casts us out of bounds, outside the civilized sphere, the human compact, the *polis*. Sex was not originally interpreted as an evil, then, but as one of the appetites through which our always latent inhumanity comes to be engulfed.

In this struggle against the bestial, philosophy appears as the point where the essential spirituality of our being is ultimately recognized. And if, in the Meno dialogue, the struggle seems compromised from the start, it nevertheless remains crucial for Socrates to succeed in demonstrating that one can reveal in a slave, through maieutics, an innate knowledge of a mathematical rule—in other words, one can bring him back to himself, that is to say to the part of himself that is sublime, to his "all-knowing" soul. The philosopher is the ferryman who allows the other, in speech, to bring the truth back to mind. But if Socrates is wrong, if there is no soul, no memory, that gesture toward the spiritual origin of humanity—if evil, or ignorance, is primordial—then the breach is open, continuously, for inhumanity to be engulfed. And this would be no accident. If humanity has pulled itself up above inhumanity, the whole perspective is turned upside down, and it is not so much excess that must be regulated, as for example in Stoic morality, but all the appetites, which then become the stigmata of a nature that was distorted from the start. As sex is appetite par excellence, its very root has to be extirpated, namely desire, lust, lasciviousness: in short, the body itself becomes guilty. Guilty of an excess that is always potentially revelatory of possible evil. In this legacy we convey the value of a body always capable of treason, a body on which we cannot rely. A body of shame.

Shame exceeds the psychological distortion that it seems to establish naturally between self and self. It comes from a place much more remote than childhood; it comes from our radical doubt about the body, which may betray us at any moment, may tilt us once again toward the inhumanity that is—that is said to be—our common origin. Sex is there to remind us that we are inhuman, that any measure taken with respect to desire is a secondary measure susceptible to being forgotten, suspended, eradicated, annihilated.

❧ ❧ ❧ Foucault, Interpreter

In *The Use of Pleasure,* his last great philosophical work, Foucault offers us a sweeping interpretation of the way sexuality has been conceptualized in the West solely through the figure of avoidance or repression. And in particular Foucault fulminates against the idea according to which, starting in the nineteenth century, society continually tightened its grip on morals by trying to reduce the licit use of sexuality, along with all discourse on the subject, and Puritanism spread outward from Victorian England until the early 1960s and the beginning of the so-called sexual revolution. According to Foucault, this naive picture of the history of sexuality, or rather of the discourse that conveys that history, actually seeks on the contrary to mask the increasing place occupied by the sexuality of individuals in our societies, a trend that began long before the advent of psychoanalysis.

> Surely no other type of society has ever accumulated—and in such a relatively short span of time—a similar quantity of discourses concerned with sex. It may well be that we talk about sex more than anything else; we set our minds to the task; we convince ourselves that we have never said enough on the subject, that, through inertia or submissiveness, we conceal from ourselves the blinding evidence, and that what is essential always eludes us, so that we must always start out once again in search of it. It is possible that where sex is concerned, the most long-winded, the most impatient of societies is our own.[16]

Foucault then catalogs the various types of discourses, from Christian confession on, that are intent on discerning the indelible mark of the presence of sex in all its forms in avowals, secrets, and familial and institutional genealogies.

> Rather than the uniform concern to hide sex, rather than a general prudishness of language, what distinguishes these last three centuries is the variety, the wide dispersion of devices that were invented for speaking about it, for having it be spoken about, for inducing it to speak for itself, for listening, recording, transcribing, and redistributing what is said about it: around sex, a whole network of varying, specific, and coercive transpositions into discourse. Rather than a massive censorship, beginning with the verbal proprieties imposed by the Age of Reason, what was involved was a regulated and polymorphous incitement to discourse . . .[17]

—a discourse whose mechanisms, implications, and artifices Foucault is bent on dismantling. Thus this secret shame, in his view, cloaks nothing other than a vast enterprise of generalized eroticization of discourse, an undertaking of which psychoanalysis is finally just one avatar. Today's media-dominated society shows us to what extent he was right, since the only thing that remains subject to censorship is this one point, a crucial one, to be sure: the point where "making love" is also "thinking," the point where sex cannot be separated from the desire to think. For within the generalized discourse of our Western economies—and I am using the term *economies* advisedly—the alleged bestial stupidity of sex, for its part, offers uncommon resistance. Resistance to what? Resistance to imagining, perhaps, that *eros* and *logos* are animated by the same movement of life, of inventiveness and creativity, that is resisted by our common passion for ignorance. The passion for ignorance, as we know, animates scholars—jealous ones, learned ones, professors—just as much as anyone else, if not more. Since human beings value knowledge only to the extent that they "know nothing of their own desire," that is, of what makes them sexualized and mortal beings. "What kills childhood is knowledge," François Perrier writes; "what kills love is knowledge. Yet . . . there is no true love except in the aptitude of a subject, or two subjects, to return to childhood."[18] This remark by an analyst is radical enough to justify lingering over it for a moment. In Perrier's view, the knowledge (*savoir*) that kills love is the knowledge in which one believes; it is rooted in the subject's adherence to the will to believe, taking the form of institutionalized knowledge, whereas true knowledge (*connaissance*) appears in the form of dispossession, divestment, encounters. And what Foucault analyzes so well in *The Use of Pleasure* is the fact that the generalized discourse about sex is in thrall to a form of knowledge that has nothing to do with (lived) sex but rather with the place sex occupies in our discourse. The sex that has invaded the media, texts, and disciplines such as sociology, sex inasmuch as it makes and unmakes even political destinies (witness "the Clinton affair"), is only a staging of our passion for ignorance, our desire for semblance, our attachment to all the figures of alienation, a staging that allows us to avoid what an authentic encounter, true love, and the condition of being mortal actually mean.

❧ ❧ ❧ Tinkering

To think sex from the beginning: *this* is philosophy, when the motor of jouissance is broken and makeshift repairs are required.
To think what, in the body, is not body.
To think what, in the *logos,* is already body.
To think desire.
To think mixture, fusion, inadequation, disequilibrium, to think the beginning that is not the origin, to think the mortal that is not the end, to think the instant.
To think with.

Especially this last: *with.* A little four-letter word that all by itself unsettles the semantic equilibrium of "think" or "philosophize." To think with is necessarily to know that one is alone and to know also that this solitude is an illusion, that one thinks with from the start, that thought is sex in the sense that it works with what is other in order to be born to itself as thought, that thought is fusion, mixture, history, minglings, solderings, seams, folds, and recesses (the *plis* and *replis* of which Deleuze was so fond). All this does not keep thinking from being the most solitary exercise there is. Here is where we are. Being, thinking with and nevertheless alone, for nothing and no one will accompany us at the moment of dying and yet, as at any other instant, we are pulverized in as many points of time, space, matter, figuration, appearance, as there are points of encounter with the other—that is, an infinite number.

❧ ❧ ❧ Blinds

If we hold fast to the notion of blind date, we may legitimately wonder why sex and philosophy pretend to take no interest in each other. Philosophy is not so volatile in its essence that it can be unaware of our obsession with sex, nor is sex so devoid of wit as to believe that it sums up all possible pleasures in itself. Let us thus hypothesize that jealousy is at work here. A jealousy stubbornly experienced by each party toward the other. "Experienced" is a metaphor, of course. Neither philosophy nor sex will ever experience anything at all, since these are only words, only concepts devised to remind us that we exist in and through language, so as to reassure us that the world exists and we ourselves along with it. Who, otherwise, would guarantee that we are not asleep in a vast nightmare? This is a possibility that Berkeley had envisaged, to Kant's great disdain, and that we have shunted aside a bit too quickly, perhaps, from our insomnias. As Wittgenstein puts it in a lapidary formula, in the first proposition of the *Tractatus:* "The world is all that is the case." Then he goes on: "the facts in logical space are the world. . . . The world divides into facts. . . . Each item can be the case or not the case while everything else remains the same. . . . We picture facts to ourselves."[19] We make pictures and we live with them, in the ongoing expectation that reality will confirm them in time. Sex and philosophy alike have often stripped them bare and showed them up for what they were: images of desire we have fabricated ourselves. Later, they will be said to have been inspired by unconscious knowledge. In its essence, jealousy is blind. If sex wants to remain ignorant of its jealousy toward philosophy, and vice versa, it is precisely because this blindness constitutes them both in a significant way. They are blind to the desire that sustains them, blind to the spirit that manipulates them; in this way they simply maintain a false reason for remaining ignorant of each other, knowing nevertheless that they do so in vain, since they embody the major passions of human beings in our latitudes, namely the passion for loving and the passion for questioning.

The word *blinds* also means "shades," interior shutters—in French, *jalousies* (jealousies). Blinds can be cracked open so we can see without being seen, we can steal a glance outside and pull back at once; we can filter the overly harsh light of day, we can screen the artificial and the natural alike. But no matter how hasty the stolen glance, nothing can keep the eye from having seen what it has seen.

❧ ❧ ❧ Jealousy 1: On Essence

In general, we believe we know what we are talking about when we say "door" or "python," but what are we talking about when we speak of essence? In fact, *essence* (*essentia*) is a term that designates simply, if we may put it this way, the fact of being; there is nothing particularly obscure or technical about it. The difficulty is simply that, with essence, philosophy poses a problem that interests only itself (or so it believes) and starts with a hypothesis that it alone (so it believes) can confirm or invalidate. That is, does the word *being* (French *être*) have grammatical value alone, or does it express some fundamental property that can really be attributed to the thing about which one says that it "is"? What is essence, then? The noun derives from the Latin *essentia*, which Seneca took to be an indispensable neologism, as no other Latin form could render the Greek *ousia* with precision. Much later, Augustine could still speak of the word *essentia* as foreign to the old form of the language. Yet in good classical French (from which the English word derives), *essence* means first of all being, that is, the real itself, that which is. This is indeed the meaning the Greeks gave the word *ousia*, which Plato uses to designate the Idea, and Aristotle to designate substance. For us, the problem of being and essence arises from the starting point of a phenomenology of existence, that is, the way the indefinite possibilities of being attributable to essence can be determined to "exist." Now, being is not only all that exists, but all that might have the potential to be, for example, a thought, a desire, a dream, a lack, something that scarcely exists and that thus teeters rather dizzyingly on the edge of the abyss. Hegel remarks that being, as essence, is the most abstract of notions; thus "there can be nothing for thought that has less content than being." What happens, then, when one goes so far as to think that being may also entail nothingness? The question is all the more crucial in that it concerns God. God as the essence of all essence, or as a being containing in itself all being and all beings, or even as "pure essence," is then identified with withdrawal, with the "nothingness" posited by Angelus Silesius and the Rhenish masters of negative theology. On the side of essence (in the sense that something might lie on the side of the Guermantes in Proust), there is the being that contains all existence (the being [*être*] of the Heideggerian being [*étant*]) and the being that is so indefinite that it becomes "nothingness" in turn. Here the gap of thought becomes abyssal, since in this view essence now contains all determinations as well as none, from the mathematicians' empty space to the omniscient God.

Philosophical thought, as we have seen, is obsessed with the desire for purity, but this elixir that it targets and whose chemical precipitate it would like to know (in the form of a "pure" response to a "pure" question, for example, what does it mean to exist? what is truth? the good? the intelligible?) is always that of an essence, and one forgets that the primary condition for the purity of essences is that they not "exist." Perhaps language can make us believe that there is indeed an essence of "pure" poetry or an essence of "pure" painting, but the artist's aim is still to give us poems or paintings whose very existence will require their essence to consent to the necessary impurities. There is more being possible in a single essence than in all the individuals that exist, but there is more real being in a single existent than in all essences combined. As Averroes reminds us, in order to exist, the real needs no being but its reality.

Essence of truth, of oneness, of beauty, of love, of knowledge. In tune with the century, with censorship, with discoveries, philosophy changes the names of essence without ever changing its absolute value. A value that it attributes to the quest for essence itself. At the very least until the school of thought running in sum from Democritus to Nietzsche ends up radically disconnecting being from value and opens up, to the phenomenology to come, a world freed of any relation to "essences." Except that—here we are again—essence slips back in where it is not expected. The absolute is a resistant figure that carries desire and hatred in its wake. Our desire for the absolute resides in a fold of the human soul and resurfaces every time we forget about it. It is one of the ribs (in the architectural sense) of essence, a means we have found for speaking of our relation to essence, of that particular hunger. Essence is the aspect of the world that is hidden, its prime substance, its reason for being. It is the unknowable *noumene*, the reality that eludes knowledge, at least insofar as it is not affected by the means of knowing used to track it down. Essence has been dissolved in language for a long time. We have preferred to reserve for grammar the place of choice that essence had formerly occupied for so long. Syntax, utterances, references ... The reflection of logicians, from the Vienna Circle right up to our own day, has definitively consigned essences to the storehouse of accessories. Of the meaning that we attribute to words, and in particular to *essence,* there remains little more than a logical decomposition in which the place of a word in a phrase counts at least as much as its presumed meaning. And even in hermeneutic thought, where "giving meaning" is a philosophical activity that seems to have retained something of its magnificence, it is through the sifting of an infinite number of interpretive viewpoints, as Ricoeur indicates, that meaning is discovered. Essence, for its part, is preserved in formaldehyde, like an ancient flowering of our attachment to the ideal.

How is it, then, that sex can be jealous of philosophy's prolonged flirtation with essence? Perhaps not jealous; rather, fairly sure of having a decided advantage over its protagonist. Sex believes it attains the essence that philosophy seeks. This is even the reason for being that sex and philosophy share. Sex surprises essence in jouissance; there—it is said—lies its reason for being. If *jouissance* is one of the words that expresses the moment in which something is given to you that you can neither want nor subjugate, the moment in which a thing as evanescent, as sudden, and as changeable as a burn makes you forget everything else, the moment in which it appears to you without the shadow of a doubt that it is better to be alive than dead, then sex can reasonably believe, yes, that it accedes to the essence of every existent better than any philosophy. If essence, as Hegel reminds us, is also the category of the indeterminate (since it can receive in itself all possible determinations of being, it must be the case that in itself it is "nothing" or "nothingness" or "pure potentiality for being"), then *essence* is indeed another name for jouissance. Because jouissance is "nothing" in itself, it is also in itself a pure essence of the jubilation of being; it diffuses in the body, the physical and psychic body, much more than the pleasure it dispenses. Absence of determination, absence of object (there is no object of jouissance, and jouissance itself is the object of nothing, neither of sex nor of thought, since it is "over and above"), jouissance is a dimension of essence, since it grants us the entire capacity of our being. But this path leads us fairly quickly into the realms of mysticism . . . "[What] mystical experience reveals [is] an absence of object," Bataille writes.[20] If the essence of man does not consist in an affirmation of his being but in the reasoned denegation of his being (the grasp of his dispossession), then sex is an enactment of this dispossession. And insofar as it purports to attain essence, the philosophical experience has, like the sex act or the mystical experience, as its principal task that of suggesting as best it can the lack of object of that experience.

As is often—always—the case, it is a dialogue of the deaf, Vladimir and Estragon on a different stage. The essence of the latter is not the jouissance of the former, it will be said. On the one hand there is the idea and its cohort of winged concepts (substance, accident, predicate, and so on); on the other, there is a "beyond the pleasure principle" that does not allow—or hardly allows—itself to be thought. The "jealousies"—blinds—that separate philosophy's windows from the pure essence of being and those that cover over the search for pure pleasure in the chiaroscuro of bedrooms do not filter the same light.

❧ ❧ ❧ Jealousy 2: The Instant of Grace

The second motif of jealousy that poisons the relationship between sex and philosophy is time. Not just any time: not time that passes, not past time or future time or eternal duration. Rather, time that behaves as if it did not exist at all, time that has been given the lovely name *instant*. Between an instant and eternity, there is grace. Sex wants it, right away, now. Maximum intensity in "no time at all." Eternity procured by an instant of grace. Time canceled out or wholly given over. At once instant and *aion,* full time, accomplished time. Considered in this light, sex answers to our anguish at being in time through the rediscovered grace of instants miraculously spared from any duration. For philosophy, the sleight of hand is not so simple. From the time of the very earliest surviving texts to our own day, time has always been among the major concepts to which humans have devoted thought. Because to be preoccupied with time is to deal with the problem of the "world," the fact that there is a world that announces and presents itself as a world. With our childhood close behind us, we all believe instinctively in the nontemporality of thought. When we think, we do so outside of time, and our daydreams are doubtless, in part, out of this world. Thus we believe that philosophy installs its armies of concepts in the frozen eternity of their appearance. All the rest—phenomena, intuitions, apparitions, images—are satellites around the edges of thought. At fault, allegedly, is the so-called sensible or perceptual—that is, deficient, alterable—knowledge of reality to which we are condemned: inherently flawed knowledge from which only "eternal" concepts would allow us to escape. A view to which Kant objects:

> After all philosophical insight into the nature of sensible knowledge had first been spoiled by making sensibility merely into a confused kind of representation . . . we have proved that sensibility does not consist in this logical difference of clarity or obscurity, but in the genetic difference of the origin of knowledge itself, because sensible knowledge does not represent things as they are but only the way in which they affect our senses . . .[21]

This amounts to saying, in sum, that all knowledge, inasmuch as it is perceptual, tells us nothing about the reality of the world as it is (or about things in themselves) but rather about the way this world affects us, happens to us, obsesses us. Which means that no thinking can extract itself from time—and that we must get ourselves out of this predicament as quickly as we can. For if time is affected by our senses, how can we build our thinking on anything solid at all, since we are temporal beings and will remain so? And it is all very well for Kant to demonstrate that space and time form the framework (internal and external) of a window that opens up the perception of the "outside" for us; he nevertheless withdraws the ideal of landscape. "I . . . first show that space (and likewise time, to which Berkeley paid no attention) with all its determinations can be known by us *a priori* because it, as well as time, is present in us before all perception or experience as pure form of our sensibility, and makes possible all intuition of sensibility, and hence all appearances."[22]

Yet it would be necessary to think that concepts also die, that wear and tear await them, that some of them already have no more meaning for us, and that philosophy, like everything else, finds its nourishment in what erodes and decays in time. It would be necessary to think that sex is not only in the instant, since the body's entire life is inscribed in the folds of that flesh, but especially to think that jouissance, when it comes, is made up of infinitesimal strata of memory and forgetting, and not of a second of eternity.

Philosophy conceptualizes time, the premises of time, its very possibility, and what relates to the world, in time. It operates in secret, examines fragments, wholes, space, categories of being, seeking to pin down what in the very fluidity of a life is called time. When philosophy conceptualizes time, it puts itself in an atemporal dimension akin to that of a gardener whose tools might miraculously escape rust and wear. Philosophy's tools are called *concepts*. It uses them according to strict rules, and it invents rules, as well, looking around the edges, sometimes, for what might nourish other, previously unknown concepts. Is time a concept, or is it only the form in which we think and perceive the world? The immaterial framework of our soul-window, in short. Time and space guarantee perception of the world. Outside of this framework, nothing appears: we have the black box of the camera, time and light depositing on the film of our consciousness a fine layer of impressions without which the visible world would not be "our" world. To be sure; but in this view concepts, for their part, would belong to all eternity. Essence, being, existence, height, whiteness, number would stand up before thought in the immobility of their pose. Might one not imagine that concepts, too, tire, age, and disappear? That philosophy, in order to think the world, has to reckon with this fatigue on the part of the words that convey it? One could object that eternal ideas at all events only pass provisionally through the words that harbor them. That on another day, in another century, they will borrow other, newer, less altered terms. Such would probably be the Platonic response. For a British logician, language and its laws form the only framework we have for uttering propositions. All the rest is just hasty prognostication, irresolution, belief. The net of language is too coarse for what we seek to catch, and yet we have no other at our disposal; we have to make do.

Time, in this sense, is only grammatical "time," or tense, a modality of discourse that applies to the real to the extent that "that" is verified and that our belief is engaged.

Thus philosophy proceeds with time. Like an old woman taking every step with precaution, it leans on concepts like so many crutches that allow it to sublimate the time that passes, the crumbling away of the meaning given to certain words, the trivialization of concepts. Who still understands the word *value* as it was understood in the eighteenth century? Who would find in the concept of "matter" what Descartes attributed to it? We are like those fervent followers of astrology who refer to planetary positions that shifted centuries ago. We believe we understand the same realities behind the same words. We think that the concepts unearthed during the Greek dawn of philosophy have not budged for two millennia, like statuary frozen in an eternal beginning. How can we understand the Heraclitan *polemos,* when terms such as *war, combat,* or *confrontation* designate such different realities? Translation is not simply a matter of dealing with a foreign language; it inhabits concepts from the outset. When we undertake to do philosophy the way we take cuttings from a rosebush, we are working with friable concepts that we translate from a specific language, from a specific epoch, into our own time, our own way of being and acting, our own singular transhumance. In other words, we uproot them, continually. This is indeed what keeps any work of thought alive. For otherwise, philosophical gardening would be definitive. No seasons or years, no frost, no waiting, no flowering. A thought would exhaust the possibilities of a concept that it had used and abused to the point of rendering any soil sterile, once and for all.

And what does this have to do with sex and jealousy? We were speaking of time, of the desire for apocalypse that inhabits any philosophical system: the desire to insert the pitons in the vertical rock face once and for all, like so many concepts that would not give way under the weight of the climber, the desire to build a magic ladder that would allow us to reach the belvedere, the "true" vantage point for viewing the world. No one believes any longer in such a fiction. But nostalgia lingers, nostalgia for a way of thinking about being that would not itself be subject to alteration by time or to the vicissitudes of existence. This would be the first piece of the puzzle through which something of the true essence of the world would be revealed. Since it is the truth that we are seeking, after all. Even when we no longer believe in truth.

Of what, in sex, can philosophy be jealous, caught up as it is in the meanderings of concepts for which it spends an infinite amount of time shoring up justifications? What philosophy envies in sex is something quite simple, something it intuits (and this is philosophy, which proceeds only step by step and not in lightning-like bursts, at least not often): it envies the *kairos,* the instant of decision, the right moment, the bull's-eye. In Sophocles and Homer, the *kairos* is the moment when the archer strikes the heart. The Greeks invented this extraordinary little word to express the opportune moment, the instant when everything shifts, the event that takes place. The *kairos* is the here and now deployed absolutely. Except that there's a catch: just as thinking the present puts us in the position of embracing the past and the future and weaving knots around them without ever being able to pin down the status of "now," since "now" is already no longer, in the same way, the *kairos* can be grasped only in the act. At the very point where thinking rejoins action and becomes wholly an event. The *kairos* is a sort of fold, Deleuze would say. It is in the place of the fold that a line appears on the paper, a wrinkle, neither crooked nor straight—a line that cannot be prevented from appearing. The same thing holds true for the *kairos.* Some have objected that it was too easy to name, just like that, something so tenuous that it could be seen only after the fact. Something ungraspable by nature, inevitable afterward for anyone who turns around to contemplate what has taken place. Because one never knows what has really happened. Even if there were witnesses, they would not be able to say anything about it, or not very much. Who is *there* when something takes place? Who can really coincide with the instant, or rather with the event in the instant when "it" happens? You would have to be transparent, egoless, the world would have to echo you without the slightest layer of fear or inhibition or avoidance between you and the given instant, since the property of the instant is to be given to you.

Does sex realize the *kairos?* The right moment, the perfect instant? Does sex grant us plenitude in the instant? Our desire to merge, to become one, to forget everything with the other finds its ideal in this experience of the *kairos.* It is the desire for one's very self to dissolve into something else that would be the world itself, its whiteness, a blind space in which you and I have disappeared from the scene, together. "You higher men, do learn this, joy wants eternity. Joy wants the eternity of *all* things, *wants deep, wants deep eternity,*" Nietzsche wrote in *Zarathustra.*[23] The realized instant stops time, as trauma freezes time for all the descendance to come.

But sex is not outside of time. No more than thought is. Sex is in time, caught up in time's glue from the outset: expectation, desire, delay, regret, avoidance, failure, pleasure, difference, caress, absence—everything speaks to us of time that passes too quickly or too slowly but that does pass; everything speaks of the lag that accentuates and figures the very space there is between you and me. Sex is caught up in human time in all its forms, yes, and it is also the *kairos.* Sex is another name for the *kairos,* for that event of a pure present, of pure presence, which takes place only once and does not begin again, whose very pleasure lies in not ceasing to want to begin again, in being the repetition of the same gestures, the same rituals, the same minuscule words lodged in that place of desire where they encounter terror and surmount it, every time, imperceptibly. The other name for the *kairos* is that precise moment when desire ceases to be desire and comes undone as it becomes embodied.

❦ ❦ ❦ Jealousy 3: On Truth

Truth, for the philosopher, has the value of life, the value of an act. The exemplarity of the philosophical life lived in authenticity is what makes thought something other than an imaginary deployment. The truth of a certain relation to knowledge, a relation of desire and astonishment, of hunger—in the most radical sense of the word—is what makes a work of philosophy. Otherwise, we think in vain. The history of ideas, the study of metaphysics, ontology, and other logics will never cause a desire for truth to be embodied in a thought. For that, the philosophic work has to be born of the hunger, the desire for truth, that straddles, so to speak, the sole destiny of an individual. Thought has to meet the living at the precise place in which desire, and thus truth, is produced. On the thread of such a desire, one unfailingly encounters sexuality. Not de facto, as a consequence of an authentic philosophic life (such a life could be chaste, after all), but because sex is the laying bare of such a desire, a desire to know that does not stop at the skin or at pleasure or pain, a desire that is not limited to the complex machinery of the instincts—sex is a movement of pure consciousness. Two lovers making love will go as far as they can in their search for the nudity of the other, not under the skin, or even in regions of blood, not in any extremity of the body, but in the place where desire is born, where knowledge of dreams operates in secret, where the space of a name that becomes love is hollowed out, where jouissance itself keeps still.

For Jan Patočka, our responsibility as beings is engaged in this struggle for truth (he himself paid for it with his life), because truth, in the first place, is constitutive of our humanity. If we abandon that quest, our own human condition will remain pending, in sufferance. "In sufferance" also characterizes an exile, a desertion, a place that we no longer inhabit. Even if the absolute value of truth is denied, even if truth is only a false version of the ideal, there remains in us the indelible mark of its passage inasmuch as it affects our thought, our acts, our very being.

Sex, in all the time it takes to love desire caress lick bite penetrate distance deafen extenuate, in all the deployed dimension of desire, sex seeks truth in a place where the body tells no lies, a place where the body abandons itself so fully, so wholly, that something can begin. Because true beginnings are rare and because a beginning belongs to truth. A truth that cannot be narrated, cannot be wrecked by hasty reasons, excuses, or pretexts. At the beginning, one does not lie. One is held fast to authenticity. Despite oneself or beyond oneself, that depends. Truth, in this sense, is always given. It is a donation of being, since it contains being, for if being were not "true" nothing else would be true either; there would be only fullness and emptiness, without resonance, without fractures, without forgetting. The truth is given as soon as there is a beginning and an encounter, in a place where there is being—that is to say, where we are traversed well beyond the "I" or the "you" or even the "we." In an encounter, one is terrified, overcome. Whether the encounter involves a concept, a face, a memory, or a gesture. To encounter is to make space for the other, inasmuch as the other infinitely exceeds the place where it is expected. To begin is to be there wholly. To be there. In the beginning, we do not evade. We are caught up entirely in the living movement of what is beginning right there where we are, and we are led to be still more intensely alive.

To philosophize is to seek what is true, perhaps; but it is especially to be in relation with the gift of truth that belongs to beginnings and encounters. When thought advances in its nakedness and proceeds toward an encounter, then thought is, in this sense, sexual. To this all Plato's dialogues bear witness.

Sex, philosophy: both desire what is true. True as a declension of the expectation of truth, as a moment of that awaiting. Sexuality is said to be (perhaps?) the most precise indicator of our internal makeup, quite simply of our being. In jouissance, truth and the subject make a single body; truth carries the subject away to a place where the latter can no longer pretend or lie, can no longer go back on his or her word. In this so scarcely corporeal country that philosophy traverses in pursuit of meaning, where does truth reside? For the philosopher, what is the act of contemplation (Aristotle) that will give value to truth? What jubilation will be its revelation?

Nietzsche sets the tone in the lapidary style of one of his posthumous fragments: "1. Truth as a cloak for completely different impulses and drives. 2. The pathos of truth is related to *belief*. 3. The drive for lies fundamental. 4. Truth is unknowable. Everything knowable semblance. Significance of art as truthful semblance."[24] There is no way to put it more clearly. Truth is an unhealthy passion of the human soul, and thus of metaphysics. But this passion cannot be removed without risking the decomposition of life itself. Because the response we give to our belief in truth is creative, because this is how we deploy a world. But if Nietzsche has a passionate relation to truth as a necessary illusion, the same cannot be said of other philosophers. In the West, the search for truth remains the cornerstone of philosophy, remains what philosophy has opposed to all other forms of "approximate" knowledge, what it has envied in science, what it has been jealous of in religion. Even hermeneutics would not survive without an index of value allotted to truth. To interpret, translate, displace, imagine, create, is still to think. Still, the fact remains that thinking is a matter of shedding light on an indistinct road while we cling to some magic lantern, a matter of glimpsing some morality, however precarious; a matter of providing support to the cogwheels of understanding. The desire for truth, then, would belong to philosophical research and sexual jouissance alike, with equal intensity; the one could only envy the other the privileged access to the truth of which it would like to be the sole possessor. To desire the true, the "raw," the "skinned," the skeleton, the heart of reality, is to do the work of the slaughterhouse. Yes, sex also loves gentleness, sensuality, illusion. So does thought, Nietzsche retorts. We think we want truth, and we shall continue to cling to that illusion, to its sweetness, its voluptuousness.

❦ ❦ ❦ Dionysian Life

From Plato to Jan Patočka, sex has been perceived as *furor* and rapture, a state of being drawn outside the self. The Dionysian dimension of all passion traversed the civilization of ancient Greece from the earliest beginnings of its mythological corpus. The figures of Dionysus and the Bacchanalia crystallize the entire set of orgiastic motifs, from collective fury to the carrying away of bodies and their furious dismemberment: the reign of what is too close, blended, confused—generations, the dead and the living, the animal and the human, the sacred and the profane. The god Dionysus explodes all notions of identity with the self. He flees by transforming himself; he appears under multiple masks, and he drags the Bacchantes along with him in his madness, in a cortege given over to carnage and orgies; his identity is multiple in his very body. Part demon, part man, part god, he is pursued by the goddess Hera, who wants to put him to death because he subverts the order of the living and the dead, thus also that of memory. He inhabits the tragic dimension par excellence. Through the figure of the god Pan and other avatars, we see Dionysian sexuality displayed on stage—on all stages—as a device for knowing and overturning identity. Dionysus is excess, disproportion, the indecency of truth laid bare, spewing forth, carnivalesque. In the face of the ideal, this extravagance maintains the reality of the erotic body, the desiring body, as the sole measure of a different—and radical—truth that stands as an obstacle to the separation between death and life, between memory and future, between representation and will. But in this movement of discordance and dismembering, in the Dionysian dance, we find creative forces spouting up from the body itself, from its flesh, its guts, its cries, its blood, its womb. This enigmatic matricial reality is assembled by the god's multiple identities; this is the point of opening and passage between the living and the dead at which sex and generation, jouissance and ecstasy, are articulated. But Dionysus is a dangerous god, radically foreign to the order deployed by the world according to the *logos*. And the attraction of the pleasure of bodies remains the principal threat to philosophers, the distraction most likely to deflect them from the quest for truth.

In his *Heretical Essays,* Patočka reminds us that the myth of Plato's cave is a reversal of the traditional mysteries and their orgiastic cults. Those cults already aimed if not at a fusion, then at least at a confrontation of the responsible and the orgiastic. The cave is a remnant of the subterranean gathering place of the mysteries; it is the womb of Earth Mother. Plato's novel idea is the will to leave the womb of Earth Mother and to follow the pure "path of light" . . . Responsibility triumphs over the orgiastic [in Platonic doctrine], incorporates it as a subordinate moment, as *Eros* which cannot understand itself until it understands that its origin is not in the corporeal world, in the cave, but rather that it is only a means for the ascent to the Good with its absolute claim and its hard discipline.[25]

The Dionysian dimension is par excellence that of metamorphosis, which liberates the possibility of the exceptional. When we are in the "exceptional" mode (as opposed to the ordinary, the everyday), Patočka writes,

we are *enraptured,* something more powerful than our free possibility, our responsibility, seems to break into our life and bestow on it meaning which it would not know otherwise . . . Here we are not escaping from ourselves, but, rather, we are surprised by something, taken aback, captivated by it, and that something does not belong among things and in the ordinary day in which we can lose ourselves among the things that preoccupy us. Here we experience the world not only as the region of what is in our power but also as what opens itself up to us *of* itself and, as experience (for instance, of the erotic, of the sexual, of the demonic, of the dread of the holy), is then capable of penetrating and transforming our life.[26]

This experience of the erotic is not separate from life, it can diffuse and transform our life. It is the chronicle of this "real life" that needs to be exhumed and for which philosophical thought also bears responsibility.

❧ ❧ ❧ Rhythms

In sex can be found the history of a cry, a rhythm, a syncope, a word wrenched from the body, scorched by jouissance. It is the history of the rhythms that crop up in speech well below the level of words but that constitute the history of speech, its soul, as is said of the very fine threads wound around a thousand times inside the sheath of a rope and that may break without appearing to weaken the strand. This rhythm is the intimate order of thought, its silent architecture, its reason for being, as in all true literature.

Merleau-Ponty puts it this way: "my body and the other person's are one whole, two sides of one and the same phenomenon, and the anonymous existence of which my body is the ever-renewed trace henceforth inhabits both bodies simultaneously."[27] These two sides of the same phenomenon cause a sequence, a musical scansion, to appear; where the body begins and ends is where speech begins and ends. The whole history of literature is about rendering this rhythm, making it give up what it has swallowed, as it were, so that the rhythm can charge the text with something other than the meaning of a word, a sentence, a story. Philosophy has exiled itself once and for all from the question of rhythm and of all "literature," the literature that is first of all a rhythm, a step. Literature as the genius of spacing within speech, between words, within words, on the page, words that come to scan silence, to stop it. Concerning this literature, philosophy can only gloss, interpret, divert its aim, as Deleuze did with such virtuosity. And yet one may wonder why rhythm is present as soon as there is thought. Rhythm (that is, literature) inhabits thought like a matrix prerequisite to all thought. Locked within all literature there is a cry, there is speech extracted by force from silence or from screams. But literature cannot accede directly to this speech either through meaning or through language. Philosophy, for its part, has taken up a position in the vicinity of this muted music; it can neither join in the music nor stifle the sound, since philosophy, too, as language, has its origins in that same music. What philosophy envies in sex is precisely the fact that sex inhabits this rhythm. Nothing structures sex but the primordial relation to rhythm—body, skin, blood, mixtures, salivas, suffering, pleasure—that contains the initial pulsation of the living. In the place where speech is born, in the place where the earliest stammering mingles with the body and with the world, with the mother and with matter.

If philosophy has conceived of itself as a prolegomenon to discourse about the world and reality as a whole, prior to all other discourse, this is because it seeks to situate itself at the origin of human questioning. At the place where one interrogates the very first things. I—you—world—being—value—beauty—and so on. Yet in the beginning there is rhythm, there is a pulsation that inscribes difference in unity. The earliest scansions—empty/full, silence/noise, light/darkness, I/you—preside over every genesis.

❧ ❧ ❧ On the Political: Sade in the Boudoir

When there is no question of jealousy between sex and philosophy, silence descends on the bedroom with half-closed blinds. Interaction between sex and philosophy is dangerous; indeed, it is preferable to believe that they have not yet met. "The strongest and most evil spirits have so far done the most to advance humanity: again and again they relumed the passions that were going to sleep—all ordered society puts the passions to sleep—..."[28] There is another reason for the theoretical philosophical corpus to consign sex to secrecy, and that is the subversive charge that sexuality inscribes in political space.

But political space is also the space in which revolutions germinate. And sex and philosophy alike have to do, in different ways, with revolution. When Sade interrupts his pamphlet with the exhortation "Frenchmen, yet another effort if you want to be republicans,"[29] he is signifying in advance of Freud and Lacan that thought is a sublimation of sex, about which it wants to "know" nothing. Sublimation, or what Lacan, after Descartes, articulates differently: "I think there where I am not." Because where I am, where "I" at least think I am, is precisely in a space that already belongs to the political, where the other has the right of oversight with respect to me, where I come to terms with the other in a coherent way, without being able to disengage myself from what is provoked by this relationship that begins with three, as soon as there is a third party as witness. But let us return to Sade, who has the persistent audacity to situate revolutionary discourse at the precise spot where the erotic scene is on the verge of taking place. Moreover, with Sade, everything is already anticipated, this will happen, and that; he exploits the theatrical effect of announcing orgies, spectacles, and other atrocities, but when it comes down to the description of the thing itself, the matter is expedited in a few paragraphs or even just a few sentences. The staging is designed for anticipation and cuts. The cutting effect, then, of the political. It is always for a desire that one struggles or dies, Lacan maintains, not without irony. The freedom claimed here is a new factor (as Sade states), not inasmuch as it inspires a revolution, but because it transports that revolution onto the altar of desire. Yet how far does Sade go in the experience of that jouissance, or of its truth? What is articulated is ordinarily understood, if not appreciated, as a mystification. Let us say that Sade's proposition reverses Kant's universal morality, point for point, in the following terms: "I have the right to enjoy your body, anyone may say to me, and I shall exercise that right, without any limit that might stop me, according to the whim of the demands that my tastes lead me to make." "Such is the rule," Lacan comments, "in which one claims to submit the will of all, as soon as a society puts it into effect by its constraint."[30] Kantian or neo-Kantian rational discourse—in short, discourse that stems from the Enlightenment inasmuch as it is necessarily articulated with political thought, that is, with the question of "how to live together"—implicitly establishes the hypothesis that it is possible to escape Hobbes's pessimism or Machiavelli's cynicism. Sade heaps scorn on this *humanist* hypothesis, but without ever renouncing the humanist ideal that sees in every man a being of reason and law. For the tutelary rule of discourse remains, the rule common to all—the rule according to which philosophical discourse is a tool of the political. In other words, it is not because reason, in Sade's text, turns out to be in thrall to the pleasure of manipulating pleasure, as well as charged with making apparent in vice the only truth that acknowledges the murderous drives lodged within every one of us, that reason nevertheless renounces its prerogatives.

For philosophical thought is a discourse that presents itself first of all as a weapon of persuasion. In Plato's dialogues, there is always someone who seeks to reduce the adversary to silence with the help of the highly precise instrument we know as the *logos,* an instrument that ought to be common to all. Socrates not only does not answer his interlocutors, he refers them to knowledge that we would call "unconscious" today, knowledge that embodies the only way in which one can free oneself from error, illusion, the enslavement of the senses, ignorance, and so on. A freeing that cannot be separated from the status of citizen and free man. In this sense, philosophical language, unlike all other languages, is doubly political: it is political because it is inscribed in the polity, but also because it operates in the space of confrontation. Socrates, Plato, and Aristotle are conceivable only in the polity, the *polis.* Inasmuch as the dimension of the political is the necessary passage between discourse and war, between *logos* and *polemos,* or confrontation, it uses force or ruse and can do without reason. The Italian philosopher Vico reminds us that *polemos* has the same root as *polis.* In fact, the polity is the place of conflict, but it is also the place of hospitality. This connection is established by etymology: in Latin, the terms *hospes* and *hostis* are the same.[31] The *hospes,* the host or guest, the one who gives or to whom one gives hospitality, is also, etymologically, the one who is hostile to me. Armed with the *logos,* philosophy, as its name indicates, is also love, *philia,* but that love, if it is a will to possess, also presents itself as *eros aoikos,* love without refuge and without possession.

Sade explores the dissident, overexposed path along the road by which rational discourse becomes perverse and destroys the possibility of speech, oaths, and hospitality from within, turning it into a weapon of persecution and murder. This discourse is then transformed into an instrument of enjoyment of the other, who is reduced to the status of pure object. Of philosophical *philia,* of the *eros aoikos* that inhabits all thought inasmuch as it opens up the space of the political and the space of hospitality simultaneously, there is no more question. Philosophical reason in Sade's discourse is a mirror image, so to speak, of its own political capacity. And the politics of bodies that is deployed in Sade's work is a virtuoso instrumentalization of our inability to represent to ourselves the limits of evil, in the case in point at the very site where the political ideal of the Enlightenment was defeated. Sade uses sex as the "other" of politics, that is, as an eternally reiterated, repetitive figure of power in all its forms, convoking philosophical reason to the site of its defeat but convoking it to speak out *even so.*

❧ ❧ ❧ The Practice of Insomnia

"With regard to something in which the individual person has only himself to deal with, the most one person can do for another is to unsettle him," according to Søren Kierkegaard,[32] author of the masterful *Diary of a Seducer,* a text that describes in minute detail the seduction and subsequent abandonment of a girl in a philosophical staging that is all the more cruel in its lucidity in that it concerns the author, his own life and his vocation. When he was twenty, a gesture meant to curse the memory of his father, in the countryside, had thrust him forever into exile in the inhospitable landscapes of anguish, as in those Carl Dreyer films that show haunted characters heading off to some obscure refuge in search of the peace that they have been denied. *Anxiety* is one of the fine names for philosophy as a practice of insomnia, when it stays up late at night, its forehead pressed against the window, keeping watch over the living and the dead, hoping that the dawn will not come and wipe out every trace of memory.

Philosophy is a practice of insomnia. All of us, as living beings destined to die one day, are looking for consolation. But the anxiety that inhabits us is not appeased by words. It keeps watch in the face of the greater mystery of what it is to "be in the world." Why? Why are we here? To what ends? Why is there pain? Why mourning? Why the succession of births and days? We suffer from nonconsolation. And from the depths of time we have been speaking of the depths of "night." What other word is there to signify that which escapes, which slips away, which withholds knowledge of another time, knowledge of myth and mysteries, and keeps us in the dark? Philosophy was born with anxiety, with questioning, with insomnia. It takes upon itself the ills of the world, and thus it cannot sleep. The wound does not heal. Philosophical thought keeps watch at the hour of sleep and dreams. It has to answer for the Other: who? you, him, all of you, everyone, here, now, at once—before any possible acquittal, says Lévinas. Insomnia means not being able to give oneself over to the certainty of love, to the self-evidence of words, to the presence of the world. It means being haunted. "There is a part of the night when I say, 'Here is where time stops!'" Nietzsche exclaims. He takes up the same theme in *Thus Spake Zarathustra:*

From a deep dream I woke and swear:
The world is deep,
Deeper than the day had been aware.
Deep is its woe;
Joy—deeper yet than agony:
Woe implores: Go!
But all joy wants eternity—
Wants deep, wants deep eternity.[33]

But insomnia is not only the state of wakefulness in which the living and the dead are inseparable. There is also a "viatoric" drive in insomnia: in other words, according to the lovely invention of Annette and Gérard Haddad, an impulse to walk and to travel. "It stems from the enigmatic appeal of Elsewhere, the Unknown, the Other, which man perceives owing to the very fact of being constantly oriented by the signifier and by speech."[34] Thought is a clinic for ideas, and sometimes, along the way, a thought happens to think an idea. But be warned: this is rare. Ideas move about, travel, multiply, shrink, mark an era or, on the contrary, betray one. One can speak of ideas the way one speaks of pretty women who are turbulent, whimsical, and inclined to travel, that is, as desirable entities (for thought, of course), but exasperatingly fluid in their continual displacements, their changes of appearance, of identity, of place, of time, of imaginary—without being Platonic for all that. The problem is really how to "think" them without pinning them down entirely, for that makes them lose their charm almost at once. This is the feature they share with elementary particles: they cannot be grasped without being deformed. Since the one is correlated with the other, any definitive identification is purely illusory.

❧ ❧ ❧ From Butterflies to Ideas

Everyone thinks, all the time. But thinking an "idea" requires a little technique, a lot of patience, and many sleepless nights. Let's shift metaphors: let's imagine a butterfly hunt without the butterflies. Thinking requires the same skill, the same speed, the same gift for observing the slightest signs, the same obstinacy. In the end, of course, what will be pinned to the chart of rare species will not be multicolored wings but an idea, maybe two, if the hunt happens to go well. An idea has to be earned, not that a diploma is needed, or an exceptional amount of accumulated knowledge: just a dash of audacity and gentleness will do. And something that has to do with obsession. Plus a touch of genius, finally, in the most prosaic sense of the term: not something furious, maniacal, unhinged, no, something that belongs rather to insomnia, in fact, like Aladdin's lamp. Thinking is intelligence in action, the intelligence of relationships (among things), emotions, sensations; ideas are something else again. Their existence precedes ours. We might say that they come to us from language. The thought of death, love, infinity, being, suddenness, compassion, innocence . . . Certain literary texts may be soldered, haunted, by an idea—thinking ideas is not the exclusive privilege of philosophy. Except that philosophy alone has taken up the task. Ideas belong to insomnia; they can be encountered anywhere, but they are *sought* only in insomnia. In the tireless, inexhaustible wakefulness that is the soul's insomnia. Which never ceases to outlast the night. All sorts of nights.

An idea is the dimension, on the symbolic level, of what cannot be precisely named. Lacan called it the Real. There always remains a gap between the word that designates an idea and what the idea defines. An idea may be confused (but mistakenly) with a concept, which resembles it, having the same density, the same power, the same elegance. An idea is like a character in a novel that is in the process of being written and that summons the author to put it down on paper (or on screen) and lay it to rest at last. Wilfred Bion, the brilliant English psychiatrist who nearly died in 1917 in the Battle of the Somme and who spent his life writing and taking care of mentally ill patients (see *Taming Wild Thoughts*, among other titles),[35] describes this phenomenon better than anyone else. For him, thinking is a machine for swallowing wild thought, thought that presents itself, like a dark meteorite, to one's intellect. And in this intimate struggle between madness and thought, it is wild thought that wins. But it wins in secret; it takes refuge in folded papers, twisted words, dreams, stammerings emanating from the memory of the dead. It is a childhood language that suddenly reappears. In this sense, in Bion's view, "wild thoughts," thoughts without a thinker, have indeed something to do with madness, for they submerge our ability to think them, our patiently consolidated beliefs, our ego. Then when, in that wild language of madness, or in the childhood language of some of our terrors, or even in the so-called foolishness of certain everyday words, we recognize an idea, when we welcome it without pinning it down on the chart of rare species, when we let it traverse us while we whisper its name as it passes and take care not to frighten it, then perhaps we are committing an act of thought. Perhaps we are allowing an idea to inhabit us, at least for a moment . . . and perhaps that is what philosophy seeks during its long sleepless nights.

We are far removed, it would seem, from the shores of classical philosophy. And yet not so far as all that. To think—really to think, that is, to encounter an idea, tame it, internalize it, inhabit it—is a rare act. If to philosophize is to learn to die, then night makes room, in our ever-so-"diurnal" world, for the memory of the dead, who are not yet completely dead and who come back to us with their language and their history, with barbarity, suffering, wars, alliances, and betrayals, when there is no more ego to get in the way and when one suddenly hears the echo of their voices coming to ease a little of the burden weighing down souls. What is transmitted, then, is night business.

The practice of insomnia calls out, in the darkness, for pathbreaking of this sort.

❧ ❧ ❧ The Idea of Pleasure

And what if sex maintained the same relation to jouissance that philosophy maintains with ideas? Sex—with its stratagems, its defenses, its attachments, its fetishizings, its falsifications, its detachments from space and time—has no meaning without the ultimate pleasure it is supposed to deliver, the pleasure of orgasm. An idea, then, might be the equivalent of jouissance, that is, a rare "thing." If jouissance has properties analogous to those of ideas, it must then be the case that (1) it is not subjective; (2) it can traverse a subject while stealing the subject away from himself or herself even though the subject may not "understand" jouissance; (3) it is information without which the body is unable to develop, grow, or exult; (4) it is not encountered with impunity, for it threatens the subject with immediate metamorphosis. This last point can be read as another version of the kiss given to a frog by a princess who awaits her Prince Charming. But beware of magic spells! For what they reveal does not leave their target intact. If an idea is a metaphor for expressing that which in us is "thought" rather than "thinking" (namely, the alterity of a voice, a landscape, a work, a piece of music, or a face), then the fate of this idea will not be without risk for the subject who encounters it and who thus thinks it. We become what we think, to the extent that we can bear to think ideas, let ourselves be traversed by them, transformed by them. Because thought, when it encounters an idea, undergoes metamorphosis on contact. Just as jouissance overturns the sexual order, its rituals and its defeats, what alters a subject is what s/he does not know. It is that place where s/he cannot go and by which s/he is nevertheless obsessed.

When this upheaval is applied to sex, we have a tendency to think of it in terms of debauchery. There are other deliriums besides those of debauchery, other madnesses besides Sadean cruelty, other derangements besides those of the orgy and its cohorts of sad pupils. There is that *transport*—an ancient word, somehow not quite right—of the senses that delivers us both *to* and *from* jouissance. Jouissance is there, yes, and I have known nothing of it; it has even carried off my memory. *Jouissance* is a magnificent word that has often become clinical, alas, in the writings of analysts concerned with analysis and who are quite bitter on the subject of love. Jouissance has to do with joy, the "joye" of the troubadours' odes, plenitude. Joy is not desire realized, which dies suffocated in and along with its realization; joy goes right through any heaviness, and in this sense it is doubtless musical in essence. That is why, musically, one can bring jouissance and ideas together and inscribe them in the same space, the space received by the psyche, by intelligence, when it thinks or when it loves.

❧ ❧ ❧ Bluebeard's Seventh Chamber

Sex, it seems, is Bluebeard's seventh chamber. Behind the last door, the one on the key to which there is still a trace of blood that cannot be wiped away, is a room where death is found. And not just any death! The death of the wife, the woman, the (female) lover—death for the woman doomed by her curiosity. Sex is the chamber promised to our curiosity, and from that knowledge one is not supposed come back alive. There is a whole mythology surrounding sex and death that has to do with knowledge. It begins with Genesis, with the forbidden fruit, and it is echoed in all the chambers of desire opened up by literature. This forbidden knowledge, this door whose key is handed over with the order not to use it, is the West's representation of sex itself. The delights it procures can only come at a price. No debt is heavy enough; payment in blood is required. The mingled blood of castration, menstruation, lost virginity. Of the three liquids in the human body, water (tears, saliva, sweat), sperm, and blood, blood is the only one that signifies death as well as life.

Does philosophy have a torture chamber? If the dark night of thought is sex, must one go through its horrors in order to accede to pleasure? What is the point of no return that frightens us so, on which the shadow of all evil spells has been cast? Sex is not without danger. It is an inverted asceticism, a path of metamorphoses. It is whispering in the dark, walking backward, groping blindly along an unknown boundary line, a limit. With that particular dark night comes the whole question of limits. To what point does this taste for horror, forcing, rape, obsess us? What are our limits? Why do we get so excited about the most sordid tabloid narratives? Why do bloodbaths, abuses, and acts of sexual violence find so many tranquil spectators among viewers of the evening news (viewers tranquilized by not being there *themselves*)? When desire is served up for the taking, it becomes apparent that what constitutes a limit is the boundary that separates and unites jouissance and horror.

The limit is the question of sex as transgression and philosophy as transgression. But it is also the question of sacredness. If all relation to the sacred—that is, to the limit par excellence—is lost, then sex loses its own dark night, it is no longer anything but an operative dimension of the body, its extension, as it were, the place of its efficacy or of its most manifest decline. The pairing of horror and the sacred has structured the West ever since language and writing constituted it in our imaginary at the root of all experience. It is the West's secret architecture; its spiderlike ramifications and links stretch as far as one can read them. The sacred/horror duo is a relation to the limit that institutes secular space as a space that humans can grasp, in which they can question and grow, while before them, like the shadows they carry with them, stands the immense store of horrors and sacrifices from which myths spring, and, consequently, every human act.

If etymology is not the key to Bluebeard's seventh door, it at least opens up a little skylight in the chamber of horrors. In Latin, *sexus* means separation. The Church Fathers to whom we owe the development of the Latin language thus anticipated by several centuries Lacan's too-famous remark: "There is no sexual relation."

If *sex* means "separated," this is because there are two sexes. Irreducibly feminine or masculine. Only in language can one forget this, as Pascal Quignard reminds us in a recent text.[36] In English, *I, you, we,* and *they* have no definite sexual identities. From one sentence to the next, with the exception in English of the singular *he* and *she* and their counterparts, pronouns can slip from masculine to feminine and, in some languages, to neuter.

Separation expresses human destiny in Plato's *Symposium*. One of the rare texts by Plato in which sex, or at least sexuation, is explicitly mentioned. According to Aristophanes' hypothesis, man is a being that has been cut in two and that has been searching desperately for its other half ever since. "Now, when our first form had been cut in two, each half in longing for its fellow would come to it again; and then would they fling their arms about each other and in mutual embraces yearn to be grafted together, till they began to perish of hunger and general indolence. . . . The craving and pursuit of that entirety [that was our original form] is called Love."[37] Nostalgia for the "perfect union," for being "as one" with the other, comes from the notion that we were originally created in perfect plenitude, without lack or nostalgia, in a pure presence to self of which we have been dispossessed. And from then on, wandering in search of that other self that has been lost forever, we couple in order to coincide with another and to experience beatitude once more. In *Sphères*, Peter Sloterdijk analyzes this myth of the egg-matrix and sheds light on it from another angle.[38] Every fetus, he says, is accompanied and nourished by a placenta; this placenta is like the perfect twin for the one who will become, once born, a baby. And here is where we have to seek the source of our nostalgia for the other within the bubble of love, but also of our love for the double, the kindred spirit, the closest friend, and so on. A figure that simultaneously haunts and seduces us, pursues us and determines us even though we are unable to define it or give it a face, because it is anterior to us, that is, present with us before we are an "I."

Sexus in Latin, then, signifies what is separated. What is separated does not fuse a second time, or at least not as before. What is separated produces the ineluctable; it reminds us of the reality of the death from which we do not return and addresses us to what always returns: the present. What is separated always manifests itself to us in the present, in the time of crisis, the time of the insurmountable, in order to preserve the broken identity without which it is diluted in temporality. The past covers it over, the future identifies it; every time we recompose its lost unity we take up the break again, we justify the line of fracture. Every memory comes back to us beneath the level of separation; every hope to come provokes a reconstructed unity, imaginarily healed. What is "separated" is experienced as such only in the pure present, in what does not surmount itself within the act, the event, within precisely that which happens. Sex accedes to the separated, right up to the fusion of bodies, precisely because it transcends nothing in the instant: there are two pairs of lips, two bodies, two languages and worlds, two faces or several or even a multitude, but separation is maintained, and only in the present. We cannot remember "two": we remember the other or the self, we recompose the magic placentary or cosmic unity, we call for the dream of another self more intimate than our own self, we evoke the absent brother, the loved being, the lost love; we navigate between absence and terror. But only in the present does sex grant itself as pure experience of a separation to be maintained from edge to edge within the self, as exile and silence, because the other will never traverse this ultimate space to forgive you for having forgotten him or her.

❦ ❦ ❦ March or Die . . .

Bluebeard's seventh chamber must not be opened: the fate of the other vanished women stands as a warning. No trespassing. Here one transgresses on pain of death. But transgression is sometimes one of the faces of ennui. A way to keep moving, to forge ahead when death is at one's heels. If ennui seeps through all the pores of our lives, transgression is its faithful double. It punctures the emptiness of those lives in which excitement is immediately tamped down by ennui—lives in which ennui gains ground against death in its proximity, in which death is once again deferred. No question about it: we have two essential preoccupations, sex and death; but with the second we are rarely disappointed.

Transgression both reminds us of death's ineluctability and allows us to avoid it. Pleasure won like a bet lost in advance. Time's relentless stroke upon stroke, the irrevocable event that intervenes to seal lives once and for all. Sex repeats that "once and for all" against death endlessly, like a bad "remake" that no longer transgresses anything more than the image it gives of itself. A last resort. A final limit continually readjusted. Since there is only one, and it does not belong to us. For death does not belong to us. Ridiculous, but a sure thing.

Desire is built on lack, one lack embedded within another. Desire always displaces the very thing it desires, moves it farther out of reach. And love? Of the same essence as thought. Love is plenitude, fusion, joy. Thought, in order to elevate itself, in order to know, needs fusion. Sex is that moment when desire yields to love only to forget it at once.

Transgression, often, is only a blade thrust against ennui. Against the abyssal ennui that lies in wait for us as we are simply living everyday life, life in the world, suffering from emptiness, disappointing our childhood dreams and our adolescent loves, disappointing our desire for heroism and creativity, hurtling ourselves year after year toward a little more suffering and grief. The picture is too bleak? Really . . . And yet we spend our time inventing multiple antechambers of transgression in order to circumvent the void. This is the Pascalian diversion realized in a loop on the screens of all the television sets in the world. Nonthought, sex becomes pornography as an infinite repetition of the same, frigidity in a closed loop. Not at all what we had been promised. Hence: bargaining. Baudelaire will still be right for a long while yet.

❦ ❦ ❦ A Metaphysical Eagle's Nest

Philosophy long ago abandoned the fields of wisdom to stride more sure-footedly along the paths of formal logic, epistemology, aesthetics, law, or politics. It has progressively pulled back within increasingly narrow, circumscribed, and "correct" fields of legitimacy. This correctness is a temporary refuge, designed to gain a semblance of power from the top of a watchtower that no one is expected to threaten any longer. From the height of that tiny territory, philosophy still arrogates to itself the "eagle's-eye view," the vantage point of clairvoyance and salvation. For it is a point of arrogance but also of rescue. It is a matter of saving all the rest while remaining out of reach oneself. Understood in this way, philosophy would lie outside of any possible transgression, since it "comprehends" everything. At least the whole of the minuscule territory it embraces in its gaze. If sex goes to extremes to defy the ennui of existing, the ennui suspected by Baudelaire and roiled by Rimbaud until death ensued, philosophy for its part thinks it is forever safe from such things. It embodies thought's supreme effort to think the world and thus to transgress the constraints imposed by the illusion of the senses and the misleading games of consciousness. Considering itself immune, de facto, from ennui (its task is immense, it cannot be bored, there isn't time . . .), it cannot truly transgress either the body or consciousness, for then it would have to be outside of life: in other words, it would have to maintain itself on the side of the dead, their secret assemblies, their territories, their strenuous efforts not to be in anything other than death. The eagle's-eye view is the one that comes from the territory of the dead to tell the living what there is to know about unity, truth, and love. From the vantage point of this refuge, certain now that it is protected against the chimera of our senses, against grammatical deceptions and other tricks played on us by the fact that we are alive and have desires, after all, philosophy thus sheltered by defunct voices in its metaphysical eagle's nest persists in seeking to communicate its discovery to all, that is, to us. But the voice does not carry this far; it does not go back and forth between these borders, at least as far as we know. The voice stubbornly continues to circulate from one living being to another, and in the shelter of the dead it finds no refuge from which it can speak, announce, cry out. Certain prophetic voices have crossed that narrow passage between the living and the dead, it seems; the biblical texts bear witness, and other texts as well, in other languages, from other times. But it may be that what is predicted is only what has already taken place from time immemorial, what people do not want to see because it is coming back, as Nietzsche said, and not because it is coming for the first time. In this return, all our visions, fears, and expectations are engulfed. This philosophical "eagle's-eye view" thus has to remain a provisional outpost at a crossroads, at a point where one wonders how to act or simply what to say. The eagle passes itself off as a sparrow so it can peck about for crumbs on the waxed tablecloth among the remains of a wedding feast. And philosophy does what it can with these eternally scattered crumbs. It pulls together a few intuitions about what is real; for the rest, it loses itself in conjectures. But its desire not to remain captive in the territory of the dead and to maintain itself, in spite of everything, on the side of the living, in the present, allows us to hear, in passing, the patter of its feet and the pecking of its beak.

❧ ❧ ❧ All Lives—Or, on the Possible in Its Relation to Death

Today, this dream of living "all lives" is proposed as an ideal to a humanity nostalgic for its youth. The possible is the beginning and the end without anything in between. In the guise of a past there is a huge black hole bordered with museums and commemorations; in the guise of a future there is a vague fear filled with echoes of industrial wars and almost empty of rebellion. We are invited to return to adolescence, to a time when we imagine that everything is still possible. All consumer objects, films, the spirit of the times, point in this direction. The possible admits all images, all expectations, all metamorphoses; it is unacquainted with irreversibility. It is a voyage on which paths may constantly bifurcate with nothing blocking desire except knowledge of desire itself. The life, in short, that consumer society offers us in order to sell and get us to engage in selling (called "advertising"). This display of promised jouissance is a pact without commitment, without a soul, any longer, to exchange for pleasure and power; Faust has become very well behaved. It is just a matter of saying everything, believing everything, experiencing everything. Of having eyes to peer into shop windows, an anatomy of words, dreams in profusion, and pleasure promised, always. Not long ago, a strange exhibit caused a sensation. On display were dead humans (called "cadavers") in all sorts of positions, but without skin. Less than naked. One seeks in vain a way to express that particular nudity, of bones, guts, and nerves, so many revelations about a body more originary than the body itself. "Anatomical art," they call it. Muscles "in full motion" exposed to view. Architecture of the body, they say. It shocks, but not for long, and eventually it amuses, it astounds, it disgusts a little, it will resurface in some viewers' nightmares perhaps, and then it will be forgotten. A cabinet of curiosities, in a word.

What one does not see, while looking at these skinless bodies, is "the permanence of a place that is in general a place of memory, a sacred place, to be sure, where the human body, now a cadaver, is sheltered, concealed from our sight," as the psychoanalyst Charles Melman puts it.[39] Sex figures today among bodily needs like hunger or thirst, now that the limit and the distance proper to the sacred that used to harbor it have been removed. The possible no longer wants to be told stories, because it contains them all. It is won over by ennui to the extent that its capacity to consume is increasing. Thus doll-children with overly plump cheeks are produced, saturated with spectacles and games prefabricated for them by adults already far removed from any childhood and long since bereft of desire. We also know this by a code word characteristic of our civilizations of the possible: depression. Modern depression as the ultimate rampart against the consumption of everything, as nausea before the weariness of living one more day without desire, as maladaptation to the frenetic race for consumed jouissance. Sex, in these lands so well organized for it, becomes the very figure of the possible. Too much or too little, we never quite get "it" right, and we hear complaints distilled as the times become more threatening. Thought, for its part, has long since deserted the spaces of regulated games and museums transformed into huge hopscotch courts: it is becoming increasingly opaque owing to its contact with a hypercivilization longing for reality TV and other stratagems offered to the desire to be elsewhere, to be someone else, to be—why not?—on another planet. The exhibition of skinless bodies is just another "happening" among those put on display in our time by the commercialization of the possible. But there is no more flesh to be seen than there are bodies given. Because what will come back to haunt us is precisely what cannot come back. The "once and for all." In this consumerist reign of the possible, sex is organized as a dependency, a hunger we must manage like any other, by attending to its manias, its needs, its reticences. As for philosophy, it is not being summoned, for the reign of the possible cannot be in harmony with renunciation. And philosophy is an apprenticeship to the renunciation of illusions; it is a passage by way of the irrevocable. One does not live all possible lives, since the "for death" that awaits us destines us ultimately to live just one life. The adolescent vertigo of the possible become reality wants nothing to do with death. It denies death or leaps into it by a suicide that is then an avoidance of leave-taking, an annulment. One picks up all the pieces and starts over. It is the cardplayer's gesture. As Frédéric Boyer writes in a magnificent text on love and betrayal:

> Our world which no longer believes in eternal life but in endlessly repeated moments of survival, indefinite survival, as it believes in endlessly repeated moments of betrayal. Our world can no longer act against traitors, against phantoms, against ghosts. As our world no longer makes death the final mystery of the world, the ultimate liberation, as it no longer makes death a proof of mad love, a proof of extreme love, there is nothing left for it to do but consume the product of death. No option but to betray death. Since our world no longer makes death what every friendship respects and surpasses at the same time, what every friendship traverses in the end. Our world is rather a merchant of death.[40]

❧ ❧ ❧ Pornographies

What Bataille takes to be "the fundamental meaning of eroticism" is an "assenting to life up to the point of death."[41] Is pornography a transgression of sight, a transgression of what we are authorized, in an established human society, to "see"? The visible, in this case, stops under the skin. Are genetic manipulations, then, a form of pornography? Is the display of stuffed animal and human cadavers, eviscerated and preserved in formaldehyde, pornographic? In what respect can philosophy be convoked in this territory of nonlimits, the transgression of sight, sexuality offered as merchandise, as an object of generalized consumption? Freud was right: consumer society agrees with him that exploitation of the sexual supplies the best arguments for selling food, travel, perfume, human flesh, museums, operas; everything is spiced with the sauce of desire and overlaid with the suggestion of sex. Pornography is just barely avoided—though we have not yet agreed on what the word means.

Pornography for a philosopher: what would that be? Does it mean the same thing as for a vendor of images, for a woolly minded composer, for a designer of window displays? Pornography has to do with vulgarity, with excess. Excess to the point of envy, to the point of nausea. Pornography breaks the tacit contract that makes the wheel of desire go around, the agreement not to know (too much) about it, not to have (too much of) it, not to lose oneself (too deeply) in it. Pornography exposes and overexposes the hidden articulations of sex and of the visible, right at the point where there is "too much"; it goes even further to provoke maximum excitement, something that leads to addiction, something that one can no longer do without, either mentally or physically. Pornography deliberately damages what it touches, in order to make it into a consumable product, a semblance, flesh to be viewed with no secret to unveil, no silence to respect, no space other than that of immediate satisfaction and then its repetition. Pornography is not on the side of darkness but on the side of the scorching, shadowless light of midday. It flattens out contours, crushes forms, displays the better to entice, consumes the better to start all over again; it weaves a world in which everything is available and decipherable in pure transparency, in which thoughts are readable, opinions laid bare, discussed, lobotomized, a world in which no one has any secrets from anyone, in which one finally knows what drives desire, in which one can finally be done with desire. Perpetual noon under the eye of no god but the god of mendacious advertising (but a god who is aware of the lies and acknowledges them), a god for whom all flesh is a future commodity.

❧ ❧ ❧ Animals and the World

Sex is said to be bestial. Sex excites animality, recalls it, is hospitable to it. Are we so afraid of animals? Of what brings us closer to them? Why have we labeled "bestial" what humans prefer to see in the other (the monster) when, as everyone knows, humans alone have invented "thinking" cruelty? The human beings who organized the nonstop train traffic across Germany and Poland to carry a population to its final destruction were not bestial; it would be harder to be more human, more civilized, more Cartesian. Everything was calculated: the itinerary, the distance, the time needed to quarter the skins, the industrialization of the bodily by-products, especially recyclable materials: teeth, hair, and so on. In short, an entire industry was "thought" in the service of massacre. Perversion hates animals, their gentleness, their idiocy; it would like to be able to corrupt them and it can't. Animals offer the perverse no tears, only obstinacy. Speed, agility, cries, avoidance, skill, heat, blood, wounds. Animals' eyes speak to us of an exile in which one comes to lose oneself and forget everything, just for a second. To lose oneself in struggle, thirst, defeat; to shed all the rest, which is, in fact, almost nothing.

At the place where this meeting, this blind date, is to take place, an animal is on the alert. Waiting. Sex, like philosophy, is foreign to this animal, since animals coincide with the instant of their presence. They have been granted the grace (at least for us who observe them, hunt them, or offer them refuge) of being, simply, one with themselves. That is why it is unbearable to see an animal in agony. I mean really to see it, to be there, with a dying animal. Since animals are only that: presence. There is no anticipation, no nostalgia, just disappearance, pure and simple. Do animals dream of their childhood homes? Do they imagine? Remember? Do animals desire to love? To die?

Philosophy asks itself the question of the world, that strange, foreign object that plays the role of a "world" as perceived by human beings. Philosophy has never gotten over the fact that such a thing as the world can exist. Philosophy remains astonished. Sex does not raise the question of the world; it cuts into it, wounds it, responds to it by creating it. Two people make love and there is the world. Immediately, there, all at once, and nothing can keep that world from having come into being. An animal, for its part, passes through the world. It leaves a mark, prints, a trace. It cleaves the sky, it is forgotten, it exists in the morning, in the cold, it is at the water's edge, it lies in wait, it falls asleep, it devours, it no longer exists. It passes through the world without ever confusing itself with the world, without ever lingering there, without ever resisting the world or giving in. Animals are the world's exiles, the obstacles to any sovereignty, entities before which speech breaks down because there is nothing more to be done. Their exile torments us, we who are bogged down in this world, full of it, caught up in the passion of things, of words, of all the conjugated stories. Acting like animals, it is said. A thousand years are not enough to achieve the gentleness of an animal, its sovereignty. We would have to assuage our fears in order to enter calmly into its presence. But no doubt it's too late? Except for children, their eyes heavy with sleep, who are comforted by the presence of animals in stories or (actually) nearby. While they wait to grow up.

❧ ❧ ❧ On the Body, Once Again . . .

If philosophy has been Greek, then Christian, its "dark night" has been sex. The nocturnal slope of its obsession with rigor, truth, and the science of being was correlated with a conception of the body and of passion under intense surveillance. Along with Nietzsche and to some extent Pascal and Kierkegaard, Spinoza conceptualized the body. By which I do not mean Plato's deceptive body, Lucretius's atomized body, Augustine's straying body, the Jansenists' sinful body, or the ardent body of the German eighteenth century. No, I mean the body in what it imposes on thinking about the very darkness in which thought detains it. If illusion is on the side of the body, if straying betrays passion, if sex is designated—silently—as a vestige of opacity constituting an obstacle to the transparency of reason and animating the human in the register of need, bestiality, or desire, it nevertheless remains the case that all philosophy is first and foremost thought of the body. Thought consumes itself, as it were; it incorporates itself before it is ideal. And if nothing else sustains it, in Wittgenstein for example, except a pure logic of predicates, this is a way of better relegating the body to exile in a mystique sublimated as renunciation or excess. "It is only the fears that we owe to ourselves, and not to nature, which disturb us by linking the state in which we are with the passions of that in which we are not."[42] To accompany Nietzsche for a time is to *incorporate* a text that produces excitement and dependency. A sort of drug, then. Not the excitement produced by an erotic text, or the dependency induced by cocaine, but a wave of pleasure directly connected with our brain that produces the somewhat opaque chemistry called intelligence. Nietzsche claimed that he had always written with his whole body, his whole life, and that for him there was no such thing as a purely intellectual problem; all truths were truths of blood.[43] Nietzsche wanted philosophy to be consumed raw and with the entire body.

❧ ❧ ❧ On Enchantment and Other Tombs . . .

In this "blind" spot, in this space-time designated as a meeting place for sex and philosophy, the motif of enchantment appears: we must linger over this a little, circle around it—because here sensual ravishment (touch, sight, taste, smell, and all sensations) and the dazzlement of thought confront each other in a merciless struggle for "ecstasy."

But sex and philosophy are both suspicious of enchantment, of that forgetting of self in which I, you, he disappear in a dubious fainting fit. Enchantment is marked from the outset by the universe of the theater, music, and magic spells. Enchantment suspends death. It is perhaps one of the most primitive relationships to death, or rather to the forgetting of death. An abduction from the self that cancels out, in the moment, the imminence of death. A forgetting of death that would be pure jouissance. In the moment when the soul is ravished, there is no longer anyone, just an ecstatic presence to oneself; neither peril nor terror nor ennui. The "enchanted" subject is altered in the radical sense of the term; it accedes to a state of somnambulism in which the world disappears and reappears with altered features—aesthetic, erotic, mystical. This is how it works, the mirage of a different voluptuousness in which a subject avid for ever more pleasure would come to destroy itself. Enchantment against which sex, too, works in secret, perhaps in order to maintain its standing in the storehouse of accessories. Yes, sex does mistrust enchantment. Enchantment is fine for adolescent agitation or for the Alices whose desire is pegged to the allure of a white rabbit that is always in a hurry. Sex expresses itself in raw terms: positions, dispositions, obscenity, erotic games, body parts exposed to jouissance, voyeurism, sensuality, odors, juices, saliva—here all the strings are showing, even crudely obvious. One doesn't think about holding off death, as Scheherazade does, song after song.

As for philosophy, it is doubly suspicious of enchantment, on the one hand because any form of ravishment attests to the defeat of sovereign reason, and on the other hand because ravishment attests to the fact that the body can invade thought to the point of making it forget that a world ever existed. And yet philosophy has sought to know enchantment. It has depicted enchantment with demoniacal and divine features by turns. It has exalted reason the better to defend itself from this all-too-intimate enemy. Etymology tells us that *enchantment* (in late Latin) simply indicates the setting of a text to music, the creation of a song, an incantation. The word belongs to carnival folk, to itinerant theater, to the world of chimeras and magic spells. Enchantment holds the world in suspense as long as the incantation lasts, like Penelope weaving her cloth while waiting for Ulysses, introducing infinite variations so that death will no longer come to haunt the living and remind them that their condition is precarious. Although enchantment may involve the work of illusion, makeup, or chiaroscuro, it can also take on the value of an absolute, for example when we are held spellbound by beauty (the beauty of a face, a landscape, even a mathematical formula). But nothing can happen without the body, even if that body is transcended, even if it is wrested away from heaviness and drawn into another space "as if by enchantment." For enchantment remains first and foremost linked to the powers of eroticism and to the distortions of the senses that, in love, come to trouble the clear logic of the reasonable. Enchantment is the poison of a suspect joy distilled in the cold clairvoyance of the sage.

It can be said that Greek philosophy was born because it rejected the stupor of enchantment. The high value that familiarity with ideas took on in Greece, around the fourth century B.C.E., consummated the break between the various branches of knowledge and languages in circulation, but especially between mythic and epic narratives on the one hand and scientific discourse on the other. Enchantment was precisely that from which philosophic intelligence had to free itself in order to come into its own, to undertake to decipher the nonvisible world. The fact that Greek thought, at a particular moment in its history, shattered the enchantment of tragic language and set out to examine the fundamental aporias seems indeed to constitute a major part of our heritage, at least up to Kant.

It is in the first book of his *Metaphysics* that Aristotle defines philosophy as astonishment, in a still-celebrated formula. In ancient Greek, *astonishment* is *thaumazein*. What is astonishing (*thaumaston*) is also admirable, in Greek. Since the ultimate degree of philosophical activity is the contemplation of the idea, the body's function is minimal in what cannot be purely a turning of the soul toward what is. Moreover, the term *metaphysics* itself indicates this shifting of thought away from alignment with the order of *physis*. It shunts aside the mirages in what comes into view so as to examine hidden relationships, inner truths. The astonishment through which Aristotle defines the entry into philosophy is this "aporetic" halt before an undecidable resolution that obliges thought to seek a different turn in order to surmount (via *Aufhebung*—that which transcends and maintains at the same time) the opposition between two terms. This is how the dialectic is organized. Understanding, definition, and concept are opposed to ravishment or rapture, to the seizing of consciousness by an ecstatic sensuality that overflows reason in all directions.

Is enchantment the space that sex—the fact that we are sexualized beings—opens up in thought? In enchantment, there is the body with its metamorphoses, alterations of the voice and of the perceptible. When we witness Iphigenie's sacrifice or Ulysses' exploits, the empathy we gain as spectators allows us to be brought across several worlds, several ethical orders to which we have no access otherwise. But enchantment asks us to be of one body with the world, precisely at the point where philosophy seeks to keep it at a distance.[44] Much later in the history of philosophy we find the same warning about self-evidence in Husserl, a radical interrogation of "seeing," of what presents itself to us in the self-evidence of perception.

In the sixteenth and seventeenth centuries, with the emergence of the baroque in the order of representation and with the Elizabethan theater, but also with Cervantes' *Don Quixote,* the idea of an ideal world of which visible reality would be only the sign and symbol is abruptly demystified like a stage on which one suddenly reveals what is going on in the wings. On the philosophical level, this amounts to the discovery that Plato's real world was itself under the "enchantment" of a transcendental idea that was at best only a belief. By this token, the search for a truth antecedent to phenomena turns out to be itself an effect of this enchantment—in the sense that it is what keeps us under an illusion from the outset. In his *Genealogy of Morals,* Nietzsche shows that the supreme values of truth, goodness, and beauty are merely a grammar to which we have subjected ourselves, and that this grammar has a history, thus a beginning and an end. Against Socrates, Nietzsche was the first modern thinker to develop a symptomatology of consciousness, ferreting out in advance of the great "disenchanters" Freud and Marx our need to believe in the real world—that is, our need to believe, period.

In enchantment, there is musical metamorphosis (Papageno). There is something of "the Other" to tell you that you are on stage and that the performance is beginning: you are given a philter to drink, and you will succumb to that beauty. Death is not evaded, it is the moment of passage. Something will come to take you out of yourself, to "enchant" you without anyone having manipulated that moment. There is staging, but we do not know whether it will work. It may well fail. And this risk is what constitutes the miracle. It is the gap between what may happen and what does happen that produces enchantment; it is in the defeat of signs that something happens and casts a spell over Don Quixote.

Today, we no longer believe in the enchantments so well staged by Nietzsche in his *Zarathustra*. We organize mystifications, we build the future chambers where we shall be spellbound. Between enchantment and spells, there is the crypt. The vaulted chamber from which one can no longer exit, the place where the body is enclosed: Bluebeard's locked chambers. Inside there is blood, and there is no longer anything innocent about the sex imprisoned in that space. Bodies are manipulated for the enjoyment of other bodies. One pays, one kills, perhaps; one destroys, one discards. In these chambers, everything that is done is done out of sight—there are no witnesses, except the one who pays to see and who thereby becomes complicit. The spell is a manipulation of our inclination to enchantment. It uses the weakness that makes us prey to another in order to exercise power. A power that henceforth, by dint of passing itself off as spiritual, imprisons the body in a crypt from which there is no longer any escape (Kafka's Castle for all eternity). We circumvent the wings, we allow only a stage still empty of actors to appear, as if everything were going to start over, forever. And the magician's wand has done its work.

To reenchant the world, in this sense, is eminently dangerous, for it presupposes a will and a capacity to stage enchantment. Yet enchantment cannot be organized. It is what can never become the object of power.

In enchantment, there is a traversal of anguish. We have seen the death's head of anamorphosis, we have heard the accents of lost Papageno's flute, we have read Quixote's distress, while, spellbound, we have been buried in a crypt. There is no longer any alterity; the spell leads the body toward the tomb.

Sex and philosophy share with enchantment the horror of crypts. No locking up: elevation, silence. Ravishment begins when there is no more subject imprisoned by his own echo, his own ego-I, just someone who is there, in that indefinite space of the present that is the space of every true event. An event is an encounter that has an infinitesimal likelihood of occurring and that has nevertheless taken place. Enchantment does nothing but express this, the opening of the present to the unhoped-for, to the "over-and-above," or to what one would like still to call grace. If philosophy retains some affinities with enchantment, it is because at the end of what has so long opposed it—insofar as it is *logos*—to the tragic, to fervor, to any form of belief, any form of straying of the senses, it has resolved, with the help of Wittgenstein in particular, to seek in language itself the conditions of possibility for conceptualizing the world. And because in that language, it has encountered the unsayable, the untranscribable, the pure signifier, as Lacan would say—that is, a place for the Other.

Enchantment and the tomb have in common the way they steal the subject away from the land of the living. The former in the palpitations of pleasure, the latter in disappearance. Philosophy is suspicious of enchantment, which draws it far from the shores of reason, and it is fascinated by death, which interrupts its exercise because even intelligence stops there. As for sex, it prefers to know nothing at all about these detours.

❧ ❧ ❧ "No One Knows What a Body Can Do"

When the subject conceptualizes itself as it conceptualizes the world, that is, as "object," it is on the wrong track. Such is the Freudian revolution. Because desire, our own, does not want to know what its object is. Anything but that. In the theater of drives, psychoanalysis discovers something that thought in general seeks to hide (as does philosophy in particular, referred back to the mirage of its foundation): what makes people think is what they do not want to think, namely, the incestuous object of their desire. They would succumb to vertigo if they were to catch sight of this object. But no . . . they think about other things. In short, we think, although always according to this twist of desire that allows us to escape ourselves and to keep on remaining ignorant of our own desire. Lacan expressed this by inverting Descartes's proposition: "I am there where I do not think." However, well before Lacan, another philosopher conceptualized desire and the body, the subject and substance, in a manner so radically new (even if it is inscribed in a philosophical tradition going back to Avicenna and Aristotle) that he remains today our "more than contemporary": Baruch de Spinoza.

Spinoza is the philosopher of an infinite body, a body not separated from substance, that is, not differentiated from God. "No one has hitherto laid down the limits to the power of the body,"[45] he writes: no one knows what the body can do. The revolution Spinoza brought about in the West is considerable. The austere, quasimathematical construction of his major work, *Ethics,* lacks the poetic force of Nietzsche's texts or Kierkegaard's sermons, and it lacks the precision of Pascal's *Pensées,* but it is musical—to say the least—like a Bach fugue.

Spinoza asks himself why the subject, I, you, he, she, is first of all a being of passion. He is opposed to a certain postmodern individualist vision of the subject inherited from Kant. Spinoza is chiefly an heir of Maimonides, of the Arabo-Greco-Hispanic medieval world and of Avicenna, that is, of a world that conceptualizes first and foremost the *continuity* of being, of thought, and of living things. The Arab philosophers' vision of the universe was distinguished by the way it defined the act of thought as a state of the intelligible universe. The progress of knowledge had a meaning that was at once personal and transpersonal. A human being was not first and foremost a thinking "subject" but rather a receptacle of thought and of the divine. During the Renaissance, the belief in a world in which divine laws governed physical and mathematical reality was definitively consolidated. Not for Spinoza, however, and this, paradoxically, is what makes him modern. That is why he began *Ethics* (1661) against Descartes: for Spinoza, the world and God were not of different essences. He pursued the line of thinking set forth by the metaphysician of Avicenna: the perfection of the rational soul lies in becoming an intelligible world in which is described or traced the form of the whole and the intelligible order in the whole and the goodness flowing throughout all. An approach open to the prospect of a happy life.

Spinoza was accused of affirming three heresies: God is material; angels do not exist; the soul is identical to life. The first implies denying the existence of an immaterial God distinct from the material world; the second denies the existence of purely spiritual beings distinct from material beings; the third affirms that the soul is inseparable from the body, which leads to the expression of the principle according to which extension and thought are the attributes of God. Spinoza also denies, as a corollary, that there may be an intention in nature and free will in human beings. Indeed, the idea of free will has no meaning for Spinoza, the only question for him being that of substance—in other words, the body insofar as it is not simply flesh and blood. In *Ethics*, Spinoza writes: "The object of the idea constituting the human mind is the body, in other words a certain mode of extension which actually exists, and nothing else."[46] For Spinoza, what sensation conveys to the mind is not the body itself or its matter, as Aristotle would say, but the ideas of its affections—its perceptible form. Similarly, Spinoza continues, we perceive the very existence of external bodies only by the way they affect our own body. "When the human mind regards external bodies through the ideas of the modifications of its own body, we say that it imagines; now the mind can only imagine external bodies as actually existing. Therefore, in so far as the mind imagines external bodies, it has not an adequate knowledge of them."[47] A proposition to which Freud would readily assent.

Spinoza opposes fragmentary perception (inadequate ideas) to a grasp of the whole; as if things happened to be united by external causes, whereas they are united internally through a universal linking of causes. For Spinoza, there are three kinds of knowledge. Knowledge of the first kind is acquired by hearsay or by signs (ideas and words); knowledge of the second kind allows us to infer an effect from a cause; knowledge of the third kind results from a clear and distinct conception. And he indicates that understanding is the perception, in the soul, of essence and existence; *so that it is not we who ever affirm or deny anything about a thing but it is the thing itself that affirms or denies something.* It is thought that thinks us, and not the other way around!

Since no affirmation and no act of will can be produced without a cause, Spinoza posits, the will is not free, for, by definition, "that thing is called free, which exists solely by the necessity of its own nature, and of which the action is determined by itself alone."[48] If freedom of the will is denied, the difference between feelings and virtues automatically disappears. Human actions, like feelings, are inevitably determined by causes. They must not be hated or mocked, but rather included among the universal laws of nature.[49] What men call vice, Spinoza adds, is only impotence—*impotencia*—and man gives the name "bondage" to his own inability to govern and contain his feelings. Similarly, what men call virtue is simply power, for, he says, "true virtue is nothing else but living in accordance with reason; while infirmity is nothing else but man's allowing himself to be led by things which are external to himself."[50]

Spinoza refutes the action of the body on the mind and that of the mind on the body, as well as that of the will on behavior. Any belief on the part of the mind that it originates actions is an illusion arising from our ignorance of the infinite causes by means of which every seemingly free act is in fact determined. Spinoza also rejects Descartes's statement according to which the actions of the soul are forms of will. The criterion of measure is the *conatus* through which every thing strives to persevere in its being. He also sometimes speaks of "natural love" instead of *conatus,* alluding to Augustine, who uses the term *love* to describe the universal principle of conservation of self. Thus Spinoza views the terms *conatus, will,* and *desire* in the same way. *Conatus* is not a free act through which a negation or an affirmation is posited, but rather an act that follows from the necessity of the eternal nature of God. Desire is thus not the pursuit of something that has already been judged good, for such a judgment follows this sort of desire rather than preceding it. We do not "strive for, wish for, long for, or desire anything, because we deem it to be good, but on the other hand we deem a thing to be good, because we strive for it, wish for it, long for it, or desire it."[51] In other words, we do not desire a thing because it gives us joy, but rather a thing gives us joy because we desire it.

Desire itself is the activity that contributes to the conservation of self; joy is what augments that activity, sadness what diminishes it. "Simply from the fact that we have regarded a thing with the emotion of pleasure or pain, though that thing be not the efficient cause of the emotion, we can either love or hate it."[52] In the same way, our vices and our virtues are not voluntary, and we must not be praised or blamed for them, Spinoza argues. Since the power of *conatus* is limited and since man is necessarily always subjected to the passions, "the knowledge of good and evil is the emotion of pleasure or pain, in so far as we are conscious thereof."[53] Conscious, thus, of our servitude.

In the fifth part of *Ethics,* Spinoza asks how a man can keep from becoming the victim of his own passions. In response, he says, for example, that "we must chiefly direct our efforts to acquiring, as far as possible, a clear and distinct knowledge of every emotion, in order ... that the emotion itself may be separated from the thought of an external cause."[54] We love or hate a person, thinking that he or she is the cause of joy or sadness; but we are mistaken. For if "we form a clear and distinct idea of a given emotion, that idea will only be distinguished from the emotion, in so far as it is referred to the mind only, by reason; therefore the emotion will cease to be a passion. . . . An emotion therefore becomes more under our control, and the mind is less passive in respect to it, in proportion as it is more known to us."[55] To cease to be a slave is thus to understand one's own servitude. And by that path, a very steep one, to gain access to joy.

Thus Spinoza provides us with a philosophy of the infinite body in which for the first time, perhaps, in the West, following in Avicenna's and Maimonides' footsteps, someone has conceptualized desire from the starting point of joy rather than lack and has construed conscious-ness as a relation to servitude.

And who might Spinoza have been "in real life"? Sexual life, prefer-ences, hidden vices? We don't know . . . All this is hidden away in his biography, in the circumvolutions of his thought, its magnificence, its spidery architecture.

Troubled times, nonetheless.

1632: the year Baruch de S., son of Michael de(E) spinoza, was born in Amsterdam. Rembrandt was living in the Jewish quarter at the time. Johannes Vermeer was born the same year. The Netherlands exercised widespread influence, owing both to its openness (it harbored large numbers of artists and thinkers from all over the world) and to its prosperity, which was limited only by the bitter struggle in which it was engaged against Spain. Attesting to its political openness, there was the relatively new Jewish community of Amsterdam, resulting from the immigration of the Spanish and Portuguese *conversos,* or *marranes,* fleeing the Inquisition. The liberalism of the Protestant societies in the north gave rise to a form of ethnic separatism: all foreigners were admitted to the extent that they belonged to a distinct and readily identifiable community. (Similar situations led to the creation of the Jewish quarter in Brooklyn, for example, and the African-American district of Harlem.)

When he was twenty-one, committed to his studies and perhaps destined for the rabbinate, Spinoza lost his stepmother, his father, and his sister. He was obliged to become a merchant, and he created a company called Bento (as he was customarily known) y Gabriel de Spinoza. Around the 1650s, Descartes's name was everywhere, not only for his *Discourse on Method* but also for his writings on physics, physiology, meteorology, and cosmology; disputes raged over his philosophy. The writings of Hobbes, Montaigne, Bacon, Machiavelli, and—always—Aristotle were also in circulation. Then came the great plague of 1650. "Bento's" business collapsed; there is evidence that Spinoza could not pay his debts to the religious community.[56] In 1656, a *cherem* was pronounced against him; it concluded with the following warning: "no one should communicate with him, neither in writing, nor accord him any favor nor stay with him under the same roof nor come within four cubits in his vicinity; nor shall he read any treatise composed or written by him."[57] It was serious to be the target of a *cherem:* the excommunicant lost his place in this world and the next. The one aimed at Spinoza was particularly virulent. And Spinoza was barely twenty-four. So why? The inquisitors who were interested in the former Spanish *marranes* at the time report that Spinoza and Juan de Prado (another excommunicant) had been expelled from the Synagogue because of their views on God, the soul, and the Law. In the eyes of the congregation, these men had "'reached the point of atheism.'"[58] In reality, as Steven Nadler points out, since the Jewish community was under surveillance, it took pains to avoid arousing the suspicions of the Calvinists who were protecting it. Thus the Jewish council went so far as to ask the magistrates of Amsterdam to exile Spinoza, explicitly citing the right of the *parnassim* to excommunicate "recalcitrant or rebellious members" of the community,[59] and their request was granted (but with greater clemency), for the immortality of the soul and the omnipotence of a providential God were as important for Calvinists as for Jews. But it is also possible that the commerce (in all the senses of the term) in which Spinoza had engaged was judged guilty of failing to meet its most elementary (financial!) duties toward the collectivity. Spinoza disappeared after his excommunication; he moved several times, but he never left the Netherlands. Indeed, it is important to relativize the violence of the judgment of excommunication by recalling that from time immemorial, the Jews only rarely put into practice and actually carried out the anathemas and judgments that could be used against rebels. Spinoza began to write and at the same time to support himself as an optician (his knowledge of mathematics and optics is what led Leibniz, for example, to write to him). In 1657, he is even thought to have become a sort of consultant on Judaism for the Quakers who had recently arrived from England. About his private life, his sexuality, we know virtually nothing. Was he homosexual? Celibate? He was not married; living alone, without children, he wrote, maintained a lively correspondence, and cherished solitude. How important is desire in the life of a thinker dedicated to philosophy? Spinoza was banished from his community; his texts, like Descartes's, could not be published or taught. Who can tell us why this man spent his life trying to understand in what way desire, nature, and God are all one, in what way the body was infinite and our perception forever compromised by our inherent ignorance of our own passions?

However this may be, four centuries later, a certain Freud was to recall this Dutch philosopher who knew how to write about desire as no one had before him, and who was able to construct around the "perseverance in being" that he called *conatus* a metapsychology and an ethics that are in many respects more contemporary, for us, than many twentieth-century texts.

❧ ❧ ❧ Joinings

No one knows what the body can do, Spinoza claimed. Here is where everything begins, at the place where the body is joined to the language that opens it up to the symbolic space of the promise. Because a language is human when it becomes speech addressed. To say I and you. But to say I and you is to enter into a hunger for the other to which desire attests and that never stops as long as we live. And even in the desert, even in sterility, in abstinence, even in sleep, that hunger persists. It has the shape of our identity, in a place where we don't yet know that we exist, in a withdrawal of desire that makes us beings given over to the world and to that hunger without any possibility of assuaging it except by living. By choosing to die or to live.

What fecundity can arise from that hunger? Hunger is a "feeling," like passion, like desire. The very movement of this "feeling," in Spinoza's sense of the term, is opposed to the subject who is "master of himself," a subject forged by Western reason, with Descartes, in order to grasp the *res extansa*, that is, the real. If we think, with Spinoza, that this essential "passion" of the subject is nothing but the figure of its existence, its particular mode, the opposition between subject and object as we ordinarily construe it is displaced. This "feeling," far from being opposed to acting, obliges us rather to observe the subject first as the place of the body. We can no longer believe in the existence of an isolated individual who is master and possessor of his own history. Spinoza teaches us that thought conceptualizes the subject, and not the other way around. And that a certain joy arises from the coincidence between a subject's "feeling," the initial, enduring passion, and what he or she can name, create, and love.

Our era claims to be without illusions or ideologies. Once alienated individuals, we are said to have become lucid beings, proceeding through the world with a newly sober gaze. Assuming our passions. Really? Believing that we shall free ourselves from them through knowledge. But do we even want to be free of them? Our era is characterized by what Spinoza called the sad passions. Yet, according to Spinoza, power and exigency make such narcissistic pessimism impossible. There are no desiring subjects, only subjects as modes or avatars of desire, that is, of thought. "A free man thinks of death least of all things, and his wisdom is a meditation not of death but of life."[60] The passion of the subject is the subject's own life.

If Spinoza had spoken explicitly of sex, he would have situated it also in God like all other thoughts, all other substances, all other things. Because nothing is separate; because no identity exists "for itself," but only in God. And if sadness penetrates the hearts of human beings when they misunderstand their own desire, then sex is one of the avatars of that sadness or that joy inasmuch as these have to do with the very desire to live or to die, that is, also, to love. Because loving is our way of responding to the desire to live among the living as we face the certainty of our death. This is why suicide is always an appeal, even when it accuses, even when it rejects everything, even when it abdicates. For Spinoza, being can only desire to continue in being. Suicide is a misunderstanding about the joy and the sadness that one takes to be life and death or good and evil or innocence and guilt. Only misunderstandings can keep us from embracing life.

❦ ❦ ❦ Sacrifice

Embrace life, yes, but not at any price. The possibility of sacrifice, for the Czech philosopher Jan Patočka, who was persecuted and forbidden to teach by the Nazis and later the Communists, is the ultimate site of humanity. Because if the values of life for life triumph, then no human gesture will remain to signify that there is something beyond life itself. That "beyond" of life itself is the gift. And between the sacrifice and the gift there is an unbreachable kinship. The relation to the other, to you, to the affirmation "You are more precious than I" is what establishes the possibility of self-sacrifice. When Jan Patočka speaks of the solidarity of those put to the test to characterize the front lines during World War I, he is speaking of a bond that goes very much further than the bond intimated by war, adversity, the nature of the conflict and its evolution; he was speaking about what unites those on both sides of the shifting frontier, the front—those who are about to die. They know this, and their knowledge in turn creates another community, a space that eludes those who make the laws, as well as those who have remained behind, farther away, out of the line of fire.

Self-sacrifice has bad press today. It is suspected of almost all ills, in particular of bad faith (thus of bad reason), but also of resulting from a blend of narcissism and stupidity, of moral prejudgment and fraudulence. The fact remains that when one reads Patočka's pages, one can only admire the power with which he condemns our haste to divinize life and the values of peace by showing that these serve as the surest refuge for barbarity and the unleashing of violence.

In every sacrifice there is a remainder. This remainder is at once the *im-monde*, the unspeakable, the un-earthly in the literal sense of the term, and the sublime, that which nourishes the gods. The Vedas say that the world and all beings arise from a remainder. Sex shares in this cooking of the world that produces "left-overs." Charles Malamoud, in *Cuire le monde*, shows the sacrificial process through which, in India, the world comes into being as a human world; he opens up for us an unexplored nocturnal space in which the body and thought are one and in which sex is a spiritual exercise of hospitality to the gods who are continually creating and destroying the world.[61] Pornography, when it attempts to expose the nudity of others, when it tries to force nudity and stimulate its possession, only displaces the gaze onto already known ground. This cooking of the world, which continually metamorphoses everything in an act that sacrifices, is the same process that sex carries out, namely, an act whose remainder is the solitude of the body itself. An extreme solitude. Which seeks unity once again. This remainder, however, is not the body itself, nor the feeling of being alone; it is rather a hollowed-out space—desire itself—that allows the act to be repeated. This "remainder" is desire. Yet philosophy cannot really conceptualize the remainder. Derrida shows that the remainder, in the Rig-Veda, has no possible status; neither being nor nonbeing, neither world nor nonworld, it is of all eternity and is continually recycled, but it is not a universal substratum on which something might be "founded."[62] No ontology can dispossess it of its attributes, its qualities. Proteiform, the remainder escapes the sacred and the profane alike, whose separation it nevertheless establishes. If we suppose that this remainder is one of the symbolic figures of desire, we can then say that it is what philosophy itself stages. Philosophy as a "cooking" of concepts, as a principle for altering, kneading, transforming, and reducing concepts to the point where they are forced to admit defeat.

Sex is the space of sacrifice par excellence. Because it makes the body something other than a body, because it is the place of exchange in the sense designated by sacrifice, that is, an act in which the sacrificer is no more exempt than the one being sacrificed, because the sacrificer addresses an absent other to whom s/he remains forever indebted. Sex in this respect bonds the two beings who exchange their fluids, their juices, who intermingle their skin and their breathing, penetrate one another and procure a jouissance that has no goal but jouissance itself, sustained by love. This "gratuitousness" of sex, which can be subjected in reality to nothing other than itself, is a zone of perpetual danger for anyone who seeks to subject others. If it is a sacrificial space, this is so because in the end it depends only on itself; it is its own office, its own ritual, it manages the shaping of desire from within. Nothing has a hold on sex except the desire for sex itself, nothing can arouse a man who does not experience desire, just as nothing can force that fragile dynamic of desire from within. In essence, then, alas, this is where the desire to "force" the other will be exercised most violently; this is where violence will be unleashed. Nothing will allow either sex or love to be forced; only "flesh" can be forced. Flesh can be violated, even killed, but it remains the case that sex, in the absolute freedom that it opposes to subjection, has in common with philosophy the fact that nothing can subject a mind that is unwilling to yield. Thought and sexuality alike are sacrificial spaces in that they expose this profound inviolability of beings, precisely the inviolability through which beings expose themselves to the violence of others.

❧ ❧ ❧ Hungers

If what is true of hunger is true of sex, namely, that we miss what we eat, then inevitably on the horizon of our desire will reappear an inde-fatigable craving for what does not allow itself to be entirely destroyed by our hunger. "The logic of love is to consider the other as a subject, but the logic of desire is to apprehend him or her as an object," Jean-Pierre Winter states in his admirable essay *Les errants de la chair.*[63] The response of Western logic to the questions of desire and love is to think that desire is a hunger that remains a hunger as long as it is not satisfied—but a dangerous hunger for that very reason, because the hunger experienced as desire is accompanied in human beings by all the appetites, including murderous ones—while love is a state of satisfaction of hunger whose bliss constantly threatens to dissolve into indifference, sleep, or oblivion. This hunger cannot choose to remain hunger, because it is wholly a hunger for the other, hunger for what will make it cease as hunger. And there is little point in saying to a famished subject: "If you are satisfied, you will always and forever miss this state of extreme tension and acuity, the upheaval of the senses that that hunger gives you"; there is a good chance that she or he will be unable to hear the message. Unless perhaps the discourse is transposed onto a mystic plane. For such is indeed the state to which the person who seeks God aspires: that is, never to be satisfied, to remain in the desire, delirium, affect, torment, and beatitude of that unassuaged hunger for the presence of God. If hunger is what persecutes me, it is also hunger that turns back inside in search of other forces to beguile its torment. This is also how Socrates conceived of thought. An inextinguishable hunger that had to be awakened, brought gradually to consciousness. Maieutics is nothing but a tool for inducing hunger in a conscious-ness that up to then had been satisfied, calm, tranquil. One of the first projects of Greek philosophy was to show that that state of satisfaction is only a sweetener swallowed in the guise of knowledge (opinions and sensations jumbled together) that leads to our dumbing-down: the object was to arouse a nonsensual hunger, to make appeasement illusory and to make the quest perpetual, the quest to bring the disciple little by little to raise the question of truth for himself.

But it is precisely hunger that we would still like to tame. To nourish, to appease, to nurse. To consume, to lull, to pulverize. The terms of our free-market consumer societies are unequivocal. They occupy the entire space of this hunger so they can try to satisfy it even before it appears as hunger, even before the space of desire can begin to stammer out what it knows about the Other: that the Other is always beyond all possible monopolization. When desire makes the other the object of its fantasy, when it speaks obscene, degrading words to someone it adores, it does not topple that person off a pedestal, not at all; it only hurtles even more violently against that person's inviolability, his or her radical otherness. Words tear and devour, gestures grasp, but the other is always not there, the connections are missed, always, the encounter is left hanging, eternally deferred. It is the destiny of sex to miss the other, precisely in the place where it rejoins the other. There is no difference between desire and love; there is only an immense lack of self-knowledge. This is Isolde's story. If there were no philter, there could be no story. The story lies in the philter itself, the philter of desire, of hunger, the hunger that nothing can distract from the very hunger that is pulverizing it. And the same holds true for thought. The hunger that constructs it misses its object insofar as it conceptualizes that object. Mathematicians know this; they grapple with enigmas posited as fragile constructions of dazzling beauty for the demonstration of which an entire life does not suffice. But when a heretofore unexplained equation (Fermat's theorem, for example) is solved, then the equation appears only as the antechamber of a new enigma whose outlines are immediately superimposed on the one whose mathematical architecture has just been unveiled.

Today, sex is avoided as it has probably never been avoided before, in any culture. Why? Because this avoidance occurs under the cover of a diffuse sexualization of all the consumer objects (human beings included) of our society. It is around the idea of flesh, so difficult to conceptualize, that this simultaneous effect of rejection and overexposure of sex occurs. Flesh is a nonconcept for philosophy, a blind spot for metaphysics. Sartre evokes it in a passage in *Being and Nothingness*:

Desire is consent to desire... It is in fact an appetite directed toward the Other's body, and it is lived as the vertigo of the For-itself before its own body. The being which desires is consciousness *making itself body*.... *Desire is expressed by the caress as thought is by language*... I make myself flesh *in the presence of the Other in order to appropriate* the Other's flesh ... desire is the desire to appropriate a body as this appropriation reveals to me my body as flesh ... in order for my flesh to exist and for the Other's flesh to exist, consciousness must necessarily be preliminarily shaped in the mould of desire. This desire is a primitive mode of our relations with the Other which constitutes the Other as desirable flesh on the ground of a world of desire.[64]

But what happens when the body, become flesh, passes beyond words, into the register of the consumable? Today people conceive of flesh in terms of cloning, genetic manipulations; they play at frightening themselves. But the fear is behind us, we are already in a world in which humanity will have to face the consequences of scientific and medical discoveries. If human cloning has not already been achieved, it will be soon. It is no longer a question of fantasies, or even of ethics, for in Western history science has never been known to renounce a possible experiment in the name of ethics. And the issue is not that human beings will become different, malleable, as manipulable as one could wish; the danger is more subtle than that. The danger lies in the constantly reopened relation to the possible—and not to utopia, for the realization of which in fact no space whatsoever is allotted. It is certainly terrifying that humanity may be prosthetic (human beings may be physically and genetically remodeled and healed), so be it, but the development of technology is leading us in that direction as surely as to the final destination of a plane we have boarded. The fact remains that the itinerary is not the same if one is afraid as if one is serene. If humanity lives in fear, it will gradually, and almost without being aware of what it is doing, abdicate its capacity to think, to imagine, to dream. And thus also to love. Since there is probably nothing more opposed to love than fear.

No biological experiment can keep a body from being flesh. Similarly, sex and philosophy alike awaken in us a hunger that is neither simply corporeal nor simply spiritual, a hunger that the anguish generated by the development of biotechnologies will not suffice to lock away in fear.

❦ ❦ ❦ Private Lives

As they read Avicenna and learned from the Hispano-Arabic philosophers of the existence of "philosophic hope," philosophers at the dawn
of the Renaissance accepted the idea that there was room on Earth for a
happy life, a life of thought; to be convinced of this, it suffices to read the
texts of Albert the Great, Dante Alighieri, Raymond Lulle, and above all
Meister Eckhart. "When we know that we have reached the end, there is
nothing left to do but savor it and taste pleasure in it. This is what is called
wisdom, that 'savor' (*sapientia*) that some have been able to find perhaps
loved for itself; this is philosophy, and this is where we must stop," writes
Aubry de Reims. Can a philosophic life be a private life? Is it destined
to be a happy life? A wise life? Augustine tried out all sorts of pleasures
before his conversion; Socrates renounced the love of bodies the better to
cultivate the love of souls; Abelard remains famous for something other
than his refutation of St. Thomas; all the thinkers of the Renaissance
led sulfurous lives, several lives at least, and had as many secrets. Kant's
life was ruled like a musical score; Socrates' was ruled by the beauty of
souls instead and in place of bodies; Descartes was a swashbuckler and a
seducer; Pascal loved his sister and had troubled visions; Nietzsche never
consummated his passion for Lou (at least this is what they lead us to
believe), but their friendship was a passionate exchange; and Heidegger
paid his brilliant student Hannah attentions beyond those required by
the teaching of philosophy. For a few wisely conducted lives, how many
others have there been whose intimacy was obsessed by the question of
sex, which, as we know, obsesses every human being? Does philosophical wisdom really depend on spiritual renunciation? What is the body's
share in the exercise of thought? Does thought require the sacrifice of
the senses to become philosophy?

The private lives of philosophers cannot be read in their collected
works; at most, one can intuit a lassitude, some morbid attraction,
something chimerical, some fierce moral combat, or else disgust; but
the minuscule layer of desire inscribed in those writings appears there
as if by accident, an unrealized and subterranean phenomenon. When
Jan Patočka speaks of being at the front, during the war, he is really
speaking of intimate matters, and yet it is History writ large, the History that annihilates the living and siphons them off into a deafening

proximity with the dead of all eras without distinction. In "private life" there is "life" and there is "private," a new secret fold within life itself, a redoubling within the self, as if it were possible not to live a private life, as if one had to be dispossessed of it from the outset, caught up in the bustle of the world to the point at which the very possibility of dreams, pardon, joy, and love was extinguished.

What is a philosophic life, then, finally? Is sex more "private" than philosophy? When, and where, do sex and philosophy exchange their nakedness?

In letters. Letters that for several centuries at least were sites of the most scorching love, sites of clandestinity freed of all constraint, of all judgment, by writing: a sealed, protected, respected place, a place over-exposed by publication—later—of the same letters in which thought, desire, and speech, the tacit silence of meetings, expectation, ruptures, misunderstandings, and revolt explored all possible outcomes long before bodies met.

❦ ❦ ❦ Letters from a.

Franz Kafka to Milena Jesenskà. Merano, June 3, 1920:

> I'm on such a dangerous road, Milena. You're standing firmly near a tree, young, beautiful, your eyes subduing with their radiance the suffering world. We're playing "škatule škatule hejbejte se" [a children's game], I'm creeping in the shade from one tree to another, I'm on my way, you're calling to me, pointing out the dangers, try-ing to give me courage, are aghast at my faltering step, reminding me (me!) of the seriousness of the game—I can't do it, I fall down, am already lying on the ground. I can't listen simultaneously to the terrible voice from within and to you, but I can listen to the former and entrust it to you, to you as to no one else in the world.
>
> Yours
F [65]

In the margin of another letter, a month later:

> *And in spite of everything, I sometimes believe: If one can perish from happiness, then this must happen to me. And if a person designated to die, can stay alive through happiness, then I will stay alive.*[66]

While Kafka is coughing up blood, writing to Milena every day, and working without a break in the almost total insomnia of his nights, four or five years later, a bit farther north and on the other side of a frontier that will soon prove quite bloody itself, Martin Heidegger is writing to Hannah Arendt. Their love letters from 1925 to 1928 are especially moving. In each one, what is expressed over and over is the extreme *attention* they pay each other. It is impossible to reproduce these magnificent letters exhaustively, but it is important to read them, for they attest to the fact that love entails above all else paying attention to every aspect of the other, attending to the totality that is given and that is nevertheless so singular, so new, belonging to the loved one; and this attention is no different from *bienveillance,* or goodwill. This old-fashioned, almost idiotic, French term signifies that what matters to us in the other, the loved one, is his or her very existence, the other's growth in being, as it were, his or her flourishing. The rare phenomenon in which a loved person becomes another's "sun" takes on its full value here. And Hannah, who will moreover commit herself to conceptualizing all the wounds of the century, precisely where politics shifts into barbarity, where philosophy becomes universal law, where ignorance participates in evil—this Hannah is a woman who is loved. Martin tells her, in a letter he wrote early in their relationship, that surely no being has ever fulfilled him as she has, and he asks her to remember these moments of life during periods of doubt, internal vacillation, or anguish. He speaks of exultation and beatitude. He returns several times to the meaning of destiny, to the necessity for human beings to "sort things out" within themselves, and not give themselves over to vain beliefs. He will speak to her of the faith in the other that is love and of the joy it procures. These letters express the calling back of the loving body within words when in fact nothing, or almost nothing, expresses the body, when the only thing signified is this "for-the-Other" until death and beyond, a stance that aligns the verb *to love* with the spirit of goodwill.[67] To watch over the good of the other beyond possession. And, God willing, Heidegger writes to Hannah, he will love her even better after death. And he signs his name.

Love letters, they are called. By him, Martin. By her, Hannah. Almost banal, if it were not for what has remained of them in History, writ large. With the war between them, within them. Terrifying butchery. Identity wounded (she is Jewish), wounding (he joined the Nazi Party in 1938). The offense of misdirected love (he teaches, she is his student). The offense of adultery (he is married, she is not, will be later). The offense of immodesty (correspondence published, unveiled, intimate writings made public). Extreme reticence, nonetheless. In their letters, there is the joy that characterizes love. A quite radical joy that creates a bond and that will survive everything, even Martin's silence after the war, his unpardonable silence.

No sex—unless it is there within every word, and between the words, in the rhythm, in the resonance of what is not said, in the path they are opening up openly.

Sex is nothing but love. Which is exactly why it is so hated.

❦ ❦ ❦ Summer 1882: Nietzsche, Rée, Salomé

Fifty years before Martin Heidegger and Hannah Arendt met, another love affair flashed like lightning across the life of a German philosopher, Friedrich Nietzsche. She was twenty years old that summer; she was Russian, fairly free despite her mother's oversight, traveling through Europe protected by the friendship of wealthy heiresses and cultivated women such as there were in those days, in the second half of the nineteenth century. It was one of these women, Mavilda von M., who introduced the young Lou to Paul Rée, a moralist writer. He fell in love with her at first sight, it seems. Five years of what would be called today a *mariage blanc* ensued. A stellar friendship, an assiduous, chivalrous courtship, shared voyages in Europe, and soon the meeting with Nietzsche. A brief attempt to live together as a threesome; sublimated carnal desire; Nietzsche's abrupt withdrawal; Nietzsche's jealousy of Paul Rée, the friend accused of being a traitor, too close, mediocre; Nietzsche's rage. Elisabeth, Nietzsche's sister, got involved, became jealous of her brother's closeness to the foreigner, of the fact that a woman other than herself had approached the genius, the monster, *her* child, her reason for being. Here in sum is what the official history has bequeathed us. There was no question, apparently, of sex. Very early on, Lou would elude Nietzsche's request to meet her alone. They would write each other often, at great length, over a long period, as people did then. But friendship, love, and betrayal are at the heart of what is called sex, lodged within it like a secret apparatus that orients its destiny; sex, that is, not what "is done" between two beings, but the universe that pulsates between them like blood, lodged in the space of language, of fantasies and dreams, made of the slightest of touches rather than cries, made of sobs never heard, of a whole constellation of gestures never made, of desire put into words "before" and "after," of the star-spangled time that surrounds desire.

In the encounter that took place in the summer of 1882, there was love, friendship, and betrayal; no sex, at least in appearance, but an encounter, yes, shared bodies and thoughts, yes, carnal speech, yes, all this at once, and music, and landscapes, and beauty, and solitude. But let us go back to the events, to the passage of time. We have only to read what follows.

One evening in March 1882, in Rome, at the home of Mavilda von Meysenburg, Lou Andréas-Salomé meets Paul Rée . . .

Lou's diary:

> That same evening, and every day thereafter, we continued talk-ing excitedly while wending our way from Malwida's [sic] house in the Via della Polveriera to the pensione where my mother and I were staying. These walks through the streets of Rome beneath the moon and stars soon brought us so close to one another that I began to devise a wonderful plan by means of which we could continue in this way, even after my mother, who had brought me south from Zurich for my health, returned home. It's true that Paul Rée at first took a completely false tack, suggesting a totally different approach to my mother—that we get married—which made her agreement to my own plan that much more difficult. First of all I had to make him envision and understand what the "self-contained" love life I had settled upon as a permanent con-dition meant in combination with my impulse toward a totally unconstrained freedom.
>
> I will confess honestly that a simple dream first convinced me

*of the feasibility of my plan, which flew directly in the face of all
social conventions. In it I saw a pleasant study filled with books
and flowers, flanked by two bedrooms, and us walking back and
forth between them, colleagues, working together in a joyful and
earnest bond. But there's no denying that the five years we spent
together resembled this dream to an amazing degree. Paul Rée
once said that the only difference was that I was slow to learn
how to distinguish between books and flowers, since at first I
tended to think that venerable tomes from the university were
mats for flower vases, and on occasion I would deal with people
in an equally confused way.*[68]

Not long afterward, alerted by a letter from Mavilda, Nietzsche arrives
on impulse from Messina to visit this new company. No sooner is he
informed of their plans, it would seem, than he decides to become the
third member of their alliance. Lou writes: "I recall [Nietzsche's] solem-
nity on the very first occasion we met, when he had been directed to St.
Peter's [who would arrange to meet in St. Peter's today?], where Paul Rée
was eagerly and piously working away on his notes, sitting in a confes-
sional box where the light was particularly good. Nietzsche's first words
to me were, 'From what star have we fallen together here?'"[69]

But there are some complications. Nietzsche asks Paul Rée, whom
he will later accuse of betraying him, to be his intercessor in asking
Lou to marry him. As Lou notes in her diary: "We anxiously tried to
figure out how we could handle the matter without damaging our
Trinity. We decided to make clear to Nietzsche that I was opposed to
the general notion of marriage but also to point out that I had to live
on my mother's military pension, and that if I were to marry I would
lose the small portion of that pension I received as the only daughter
of a Russian nobleman."[70] This is the beginning of a very lengthy correspondence.

Nietzsche to Paul Rée, May 8, 1882:

*My friend, how can I find the so often evoked gold nugget, after I
have found the "philosopher's stone" (what is more, the stone is
a heart)?—Sirocco around me all the time, my great enemy, also
in the metaphoric sense! But now, I think to myself constantly: "If
it were not for the sirocco, I would be in Messina!"—and I forgive
my enemy.—In sum: extreme submission to God's will. . . . I must*

speak once more with Frl. L., perhaps in the Löwengarten. With unlimited gratitude your friend N.[71]

Nietzsche to Lou, May 28, 1882:

> *My dear friend,*
> *Your letter has gone* straight to my heart *(to my eyes also)! Yes, I believe in you: help me to believe in myself always and to do honor to our motto as well as to you*
>
> > « *lose the habit of half-measures*
> > « *in order to* live resolutely
> > « *in totality, plenitude, and beauty"*
>
> *Here is the latest plan I have conceived for speaking to you:*
> *I want to go to Berlin during the time when you will be in Berlin; once I have arrived, I will* immediately *withdraw into one of the beautiful deep forests in the neighborhood of Berlin—near enough so that we can meet* when *we like, when* you *like . . . For sincerely, I would* very much *like to find myself alone with you, as soon as possible. Solitary souls like myself need to* grow accustomed *slowly to the persons they love the most: be indulgent with me on this point, or rather be a bit considerate! . . . My dear Lou, my friend, I prefer to explain myself orally on the subject of "friends" and of* friend Rée *in particular: I know very well what I am saying when I take him to be a better friend than I am or can be . . . With all my heart your F. N.*[72]

Lou to Nietzsche, June 4 (in which we see that the young lady also knows how to think):

> *Just be assured that if I now renounce being alone with you, it is in the exclusive interest of our own projects and so that we can achieve the essence of our intentions with all the more freedom and certainty . . . While browsing through your book recently, I wondered why someone like Frl. von Meysenburg feels more sympathy for your views than for Rée's, when you are, to speak the way she would, the worse of the two . . . You are like two prophets turned the one toward the past, the other toward the future; the one, that is, Rée, discovers the origin of the gods, the other annihilates their twilight. And yet between these seemingly similar aspirations there is a profound difference, which*

can be expressed most accurately in your words: whereas Rée's egoist, pushed to his "ultimate consequences" to Mavilda's great distress, tells himself: "Our only goal is to lead a pleasant and happy life," you say somewhere: "When one has to give up a happy life, the heroic life still remains." It is in a sense this profoundly different conception of egoism, the will to express oneself and to express the desire that one bears in one's inner depths that make the difference; if one wanted to embody your two conceptions in two individuals, one would give the first the features of Rée's egoist, the second those of a hero.

. . . If only I could say "it won't be long." Remain cheerful and in good health; all will be well. We are good travelers, we shall find our way even through the brush.

Yours, Lou.[73]

Nietzsche to Lou, June 27, 1882:

. . . Meanwhile, I have revealed everything to my sister as far as you are concerned. During the long separation, I found you had made such great progress. . . . I had to keep silent, for had I mentioned you I would have been overcome every time (that is what happened at the good Overbecks'). Well! I am telling you all this to make you laugh. In me everything is always human—all too human and my foolishness grows along with my wisdom . . . With all my heart, with you and friend Rée, F. N.[74]

Nietzsche to Lou, July 2:

Now the sky above me is bright! Yesterday at noon I felt as if it was my birthday. You sent your acceptance, the most lovely present that anyone could give me now; my sister sent cherries . . . and, on top of it all, I had just finished the very last part of the manuscript and therewith the work of six years (1876–82), my entire Freigeisterei *[free thought:* The Gay Science *] . . . The south of Europe is now far from my thoughts. I want to be lonely no longer, but to learn again to be a human being. Ah, here I have practically everything to learn!*

Accept my thanks, dear friend. Everything will be well, as you have said.

Very best wishes to our Rée!

Entirely yours,

F. N.[75]

Meanwhile, there is the meeting between Elisabeth N. and Lou arranged by Paul Rée—at the time, things go fairly well, but subsequent events put a sour edge on the memory of that afternoon, and Elisabeth's jealousy works from then on to destroy the bonds that link her brother to the young Russian woman. That same week, Nietzsche's sister will try to reconcile him with Wagner, who will leave the room very upset, resolved never to see the philosopher again.

Nietzsche to Peter Gast, August 4:

> *Dear friend,*
> *One day a bird [flew over] me; and I, superstitious like all solitary souls who find themselves at a crossroads, I thought I saw an eagle. Now the whole world is striving to show me that I am mistaken—and Europe is going along with its nice gossip. But who is happier [now]— I, "the dupe," as they say, I who have spent a whole summer in the higher spheres of hope because of the sign made by that bird—or those who are "not [to be] fooled"?—And so on—Amen. . . .*[76]

Nietzsche to Lou, August 4 (in Bayreuth):

> *. . . and how* difficult *has become even the duty toward a* friend *who is* now *still with me—*
> *I wanted to live alone.—*
> *But the dear bird Lou crossed my path and I believed it was an eagle. And now I wanted the eagle to stay close to me*
> *Come, then, I am suffering too much from having made you suffer. Together we shall better bear the pain*
> > *F. N.*[77]

Paul Rée to Lou, August 6:

> *My dearly beloved, my little snail—I now have a slight feeling of uncertainty when I address to you the loving words of an earlier time. . . . the world that you have not frequented very much, the world for which you are made in the best sense, the world for which you have a thousand organs of pleasure—it cannot fail to excite you, to captivate you powerfully, and also to distance you temporarily from me. For I always believe that you will return to your old home-land in the end—unless you should meet the unknown god . . .*
> *Goodbye my dear, my only little snail.*[78]

Lou's diary:

> *After Bayreuth, Nietzsche and I planned to spend several weeks*
> *in Thüringen . . . It seems that Nietzsche and I argued a bit at*
> *first over all sorts of nonsense that I still can't understand, since*
> *it had no basis in fact. But we soon put that behind us, and our*
> *subsequent experience was a rich one, undisturbed by any third*
> *person. I was able to penetrate much more deeply into Nietzsche's*
> *thought at this period than I had in Rome or while traveling. . . .*
> *The preference for an aphoristic style—forced upon Nietzsche by*
> *his illness and the way he lived—had always come naturally to*
> *Paul Rée. . . . But in Nietzsche's case one could already feel what*
> *would lead him beyond his collections of aphorisms toward Zara-*
> *thustra: the deep impulse of Nietzsche the God-seeker, who came*
> *from religion and was moving toward religious prophesy.*[79]

Lou to Paul Rée (in an excerpt from her diary) regarding her stay with
Nietzsche, August 14:

> *We are very cheerful together, we laugh a great deal. To the*
> *great consternation of Elisabeth (who, incidentally, is almost*
> *never with us), my room is visited by the "ghost-knocking"*
> *when N. comes in, which puts us in a state of the greatest joy.*
> *. . . Can such hours never . . .*[80]

An aphorism by Nietzsche for Lou, August 1882:

> *The more abstract a truth which one wishes to teach, the more*
> *one must first entice the senses.*[81]

Nietzsche to Lou, September 1:

> *My dear Lou,*
> *I left Tautenburg the day after you did, my heart full of pride and*
> *courage—why after all? . . .*
> *   In Naumburg, the demon of music got hold of me again—I set*
> *your* Hymn to Life *to music;*[82] *and my Parisian friend Ort, who*
> *has a marvelously powerful and expressive voice, will sing it to the*
> *two of us one day.*

Finally, my dear Lou, the old, deep demand of my heart: become
who you are! *We have trouble freeing ourselves from our chains at
first, and in the end we still have to* emancipate *ourselves from this
emancipation! We are all subject in our own way to the malady of
the chains, even when we have broken them.*

> *Committed with all my heart
> to your destiny—for in you I
> love* my own hopes *as well.*
> F. N.[83]

Elisabeth to her friend Clara, October 1882:

> *. . . how can one call honest that girl who threw herself on Fritz
> like a wild beast, shredding his good reputation and his name
> and trampling them underfoot as soon as she believed she could
> no longer take advantage of his celebrity . . .*[84]

To Lou, late November 1882:

> *M. d. L., be careful! If I separate you from myself now, it will be a
> terrible censoring of your whole being! . . .*
>
> *You have done wrong, you have done* harm—*not only to me but
> to all those who loved me—this sword is hanging over you . . .*[85]

Diary (fragment) regarding Lou:

> *. . . the character of a cat—a beast of prey that pretends to be a
> pet . . . a cruelly closed sensuality / backward children—result
> of a languishing and cruelly removed sensuality / Capable of
> enthusiasm without love for m(en) but loving God . . . / cunning
> and very self-composed where men's sensuality is concerned . . .
> without gratitude without modesty toward the benefactor, . . .
> crude in questions of honor.*[86]

To Lou, mid-December 1882:

> *No m. d. L., we are still far from "forgiveness"; I cannot pull
> forgiveness out of my sleeve after the injury has had time, during
> four months, to worm its way inside me. Goodbye m. d. L., I shall
> not see you again.*[87]

Nietzsche to Paul Rée, December 1882:

> *She will give me an opportunity to forgive her too. For till now
> I have not forgiven her. It is harder to forgive one's friends than
> one's enemies.*[88]

Nietzsche to Franz Overbeck, December 25, 1882:

> *This last* morsel of life *was the hardest I have yet had to chew,
> and it is still possible that I shall* choke *on it. . . . Unless I discover
> the alchemical trick of turning this—muck into gold, I am lost.
> . . . My lack of confidence is now immense . . .*[89]

Nietzsche to Paul Rée, mid-July 1883:

> *Only after too much delay, nearly a year, am I enlightened as to
> the role you played in the events of last summer: and never has so
> much disgust gathered in my soul until now, when I think that I
> could have taken such an underhanded false perfidious comrade
> as my friend for years on end. I call that a crime and not only
> against me—but especially against friendship.*[90]

Nietzsche to Franz Overbeck, August 1883:

> *The disaster of last year is only so* great *in comparison to the goal
> and purpose that govern me . . ., I need another year of life—help
> me to get through the next fifteen months.
>   Faithfully, your Nietzsche*[91]

Nietzsche to Mavilda von Meysenbu[r]g, late April 1884:

> *By now, my highly esteemed friend, the last two parts of* Zarathustra
> *are hopefully in your hands . . .
> I'm angry with myself for the* inhuman *letter I sent you last sum-
> mer . . . Meanwhile, the situation has changed: I have broken with
> my sister completely. For heaven's sake don't dream of trying to
> intercede; between a vengeful anti-Semitic goose and me there can
> be no reconciliation. . . .
>   Later, much later, she'll come to realize all by herself how much
> harm she did me during the most decisive period of my life, with*

these incessant dirty-minded insinuations about my character . . .
I'm also left with the very awkward task of trying to make some
amends to Dr. Rée and Frl. Salomé for what my sister has done
[(Frl. S's first book is to appear soon under the title On Religious
Feeling—*the very theme for which I discovered her extraordinary*
talent and experience at Tautenburg—I am happy that my efforts
at the time were not totally useless)]*. . . . I found it very instructive
that my sister ended up treating me with the same blind suspicious-
ness with which she treated Frl. S . . . [Elisabeth has no knowledge
of men in general or in particular . . .]

Exceptional people like Frl. Salomé deserve, especially when they're
so young, all the indulgence and sympathy we can give them. And
even if I am for various reasons not yet ready to welcome another
overture from her, I do want, should things get really desperate for
her, to ignore all personal considerations. Repeated experience has
made me understand only too well how easily I could fall into just
that sort of disrepute myself—deserved and undeserved, as always
seems to be the case with such people.

[With all my gratitude,
your devoted N.][92]

There is no way to comment on these letters except by borrowing
George Steiner's Lacanian word play—once does not make a habit—
comment taire, how to silence/keep silent.[93] The intensity of the summer
of 1882, the essence of which continues to escape us, is at once cruel and
savage, civilized and redemptive; in other words, the destiny of these
three individuals turned out to be definitively affected, overwhelmed.
"Our destined vocation disposes of us, even when we do not yet know
it; it is the future that regulates our today."[94] The same thing can be
said of certain encounters. One does not decide on an encounter, it is
the encounter that is destined for you. This gift is also a danger. One
does not receive it with impunity, one becomes responsible for it, as for
the angel that sometimes whispers in our ear when we are alone some
evening, taking the time to stroll about the city or along the seashore.
The angel is what happens. What happens is always an encounter. An
effraction, an appeal. Of those three beings, that summer, one can say

---

* Translator's note: The passages in square brackets in this letter have been translated from
the German. They were not included in the Fuss-Shapiro translation.

that they lived their lives in amplitude, as Patočka describes it so luminously: "Man enters into amplitude upon submitting to the fascination of the limits that press upon our lives. He is compelled to confront these limits to the extent that he aspires to truth. He who seeks truth cannot allow himself to look for it solely in the flatlands of existence, cannot allow himself to be lulled by the quietude of everyday harmony; he must allow to grow within himself the disturbing, the unreconciled, the enigmatic, that from which ordinary life turns away in order to deal with the order of the day."[95]

❧ ❧ ❧ An Unavowable Community

Sex and love are set up as opposites, today, just as thought and love are set up as opposites, even more radically, as if even to imagine that they had common ground were in itself, if not absurd, then at least unlikely. Yet it is within the space that love opens up that sex and thought can be mobilized. Sex is love, even when it is violence, even when it is sordid, even when it abuses or corrupts; it exists in the name of love and springs from the reality of love. This proposition appears scandalous, even insulting, to victims of sexual abuse and sexual trafficking. But I maintain that we need to rethink the question; we need to reconnect sex and love just as we need to rethink the primitive bond that has united *eros* and *logos* since philosophy began. Sex belongs to the enchanted circle constituted by love and the catastrophe of its fading, its disappearance. We are born of a separation from which we never recover; we make do, we settle in, we think, we aspire, we imagine, we take risks, we kill ourselves, and with all this we also love; the implausible fact of being born and being alone, of having been two and being just one; the whole movement of desire, whatever it is, betrays only this: a badly executed, forgotten, repressed cut, a clever mechanism for repression, sublimation, displacement, whatever you care to call it, that makes us invent other figures to mask the yawning gulf of the vanished Other. Some will say: "Here's the mother again, think about it, we always come back to this"; but no, the separation lies beyond the mother, it may lie beyond what makes us human, the original separation that takes place in the body and affects it forever until death: this is the reality of love. And this love, which cannot be reduced either to the body, even affected in this way, or to the dream of a reconciliation, an impossible reunion, with the loved one, or with any lack or any utopia of plenitude, but a reunion with something that has been called by this name, "love," for want of a name for what commits us thus to life and also to death, in an unimagined solitude from which we shall never recover. Thought, too, is a matter of love, love and then hate, to be sure, love and then forgetting, the creation of concepts, a whole apparatus for stemming sentiment, blocking off the lack of the other, holding the other at bay, for thinking the world, no less, and coming to terms with the essential and incomprehensible solitude that leaves you standing there agape before the endless night of the human.

We are taught that philosophy is the love of reason, reason that has gotten the better of the appetites (thus of sex) and of all violence, all excess. But what if philosophy is a different love? Love of a hidden world order, of a language that would be logical even in its subtlest forms, love of an absent god, love of matter, of dialectics, of power or of nothingness, love of what resists and exceeds philosophy, love that leads philosophy to look even within the world for another world that would express it, love of reason itself encompassing its failure and its end; this love arises from the fact that nothing in the human is separated, separated from the world, separated from others, separated from images. We are separated, in our bodies we are, we were separated in the violence of birth, but apart from that act, nothing is separated, no more I, you, we, us, all of you, than the order of things posited in language. But what violence is required to conceptualize this nonseparation as Spinoza did, what violence for the one whose initial wound lies here!

To conceptualize sex with the horizon of love as a starting point is to soften it, to "spiritualize" it, even, that is, to miss its cruelty, to miss what leads it to participate in crime, degradation, the annihilation of the other, in all the forms that it borrows from violence. Yet this horizon of violence is unthinkable without the idea of what we call love. No form of perversion or distortion, none of the most degraded forms of sexuality such as are offered in the worldwide marketplace of Internet images, for example, has any meaning if it is not related to what we think of as "love." That is, a form of bond exempt from any perversion, any instrumentalization of others.

Sex is not love; but sex is devoid of all eroticism if love does not exist, even if only in the form of hate. Hate as lack of love, as the devouring of the other, as murder.

Philosophy is a science of being, an investigation into the limits of the *logos,* an attempt at a teleology of the living, a questioning of man as a political animal, to be sure; but love constitutes philosophy's first moment. Love brought to the point of truth. Love of accurate knowledge, love of what is true insofar as the true comes to reveal, to justify, to realize. Love of truth, even when a "primordial" truth is denied, even when the substratum of all possible truth is corroded, is the movement of thought itself; it is what makes the fact of thinking possible.

❧ ❧ ❧ Armed Vigilance

Philosophy is a vigil against forgetting, against time, against stupidity, against prejudices, belief, the immediacy of the consumption of the void, against ready-made morality, against the silence of the executioner and that of the victim. Philosophy is and has always been a struggle. The forgetting against which it has created its weapons is an even more radical forgetting than the one Heidegger conceptualized as "oblivion of being," since that forgetting was the very movement—ineluctable, as he saw it—of being itself; no, philosophy's forgetting is a forgetting of desire. To forget to desire to think is a very serious matter. Here is a world in which one would be force-fed. Stuffed with false thought, with warmed-over texts, with preformatted images, stuffed in advance with all forms of stupidity. Force-feeding allows forgetting, at least a sort of forgetting . . . And this forgetting applies to sex as surely as it does thought. By cultivating sex in all its possibilities, by turning its representations into pornography, we risk erasing from it, too, any possible thought. Sex is forgetting itself. It is a magnificent, essential power to forget. Forgetting "preoccupation," worry, "for-death," sex in its dimension of jouissance but also in its dimension of repetition and constraint is a practice of oblivion. Forgetting that it has already taken place and will take place again and always, sex functions as a constantly reiterated first time, a forgetting of that to which desire is subjected (its internal, fantasmatic, neurotic constraints), a forgetting of the body—yes, really, for the body is present, it is no longer anything but presence, but not as body, it makes itself present as the source of desire and pleasure, as a landscape, an image, a zone of attraction and repulsion giving rise to calm or to violence. A forgetting that constitutes a limit to the nocturnal territories of desire, there where one confronts a forgotten primitiveness, the archaism of humanity's earliest moments, the devouring, primary, unlimited hunger for love that the human being learns so slowly to contain and to overcome. This hunger, the prototype of all hunger, is also a hunger for knowledge of all types, insofar as knowledge allows one a respite, patiently fills a space that would otherwise remain empty. Astonishment, hunger, time. Here is where philosophy and sex are in harmony, on the shores of birth and death, waiting and forgetting, patience and rage. In the hunger that philosophy distracts and deflects toward the ideal, the hunger nourished by the desire for a body that would be foreign to the self and yet its likeness, in this hunger there is time. Philosophy keeps watch with its arms at the ready.

❧ ❧ ❧ Blinds

Who is blind in this story? Why is the date "blind"? On the margins of the encounter between sex and philosophy, in the shadows that hide the surrounding landscape, there is this "blind," this obstacle to seeing, but also this word that designates a shade, a veil, something that is interposed between the gaze and the outside, or the inside, it all depends on where one stands, something that conceals the better to turn the eye away from the rawness of sight. The blind date that has been at issue here will never be able to dispel its protagonists' blindness. So they will never see each other.

❧ ❧ ❧ Sade: A Summons

But let us come back for a moment to Sade. Sade writes in prison. He writes in the failure of the ideals of the Revolution. He writes in the resounding defeat of the Enlightenment. In the Bastille, he asks that a second door be installed inside his cell, one that he can open whenever he wishes. This is the gesture he opposes to the Terror, opposes to liberty construed as an art of libertinage. The night of pleasures thrown in Kant's face, Kant with his universal morality: Do not do unto others what you would not want them to do unto you. Sade produces a performative text. He says: I am going to summon the philosophers into the boudoir. And he does so. He summons philosophy to a place where it is confronted with its own blind spot, a place where all words are lacking, where desire and its figures are arrayed, where the human and the inhuman no longer have any concepts they can use to tell themselves apart.

The boudoir is the nonplace of thought; it is the place of the blind date. Neither public nor private, the boudoir is a place where entities can encounter one another anonymously; today we would call this by another name, in any case not *bedroom* or *chamber* or *salon*. With Sade, reason confesses its powerlessness to conceptualize the revolution, whose result even so installs the worst of the bourgeoisies, that of the nineteenth century, riddled with hypocrisy, sick with its desires; it produces Flaubert, too, by way of genius.

My pleasure in thought, says Sade, lies in having my way with bodies. The act of writing is performative: writing and thinking are acts. What philosophy cannot tolerate is the nonresponse to which the enigma of sex refers it. No philosopher can bear up in the boudoir. What philosophy does not succeed in conceptualizing is the traversal of a disaster. How can one traverse the disaster of thought? This is precisely where philosophy ends, in the face of the stammerings of Vladimir and Estragon. "What are we doing here? Waiting. Waiting for whom? Waiting for Godot." It may be that traversing the impossibility of the relation to sex is what founds philosophy. The black sun of thought about sex. Sex is what leads to traversal, to exile; it orients and disorients. From this exile, literature is born. Literature is the other, hidden guest at this blind date in the boudoir.

❧ ❧ ❧ Mortal Condition (of Literature)

The condition of man is to be mortal, it is said. But the moments when a being, whatever it may be, wherever it may come from, conceptualizes itself, knows itself to be mortal, are rare. So rare that by ricocheting to the surface of the existence of the one who, abruptly, recalls them, they form a circle that spreads out and finally breaks apart. This is what happens with sudden, shattering illuminations; like the sea, they have a horizon that looks immobile, and they keep us in life up to the last second. We live oblivious to the promise to be unto death, as if we could remain this way forever, with the intimate perception left over from childhood that time is ultimately on our side, that it is in us and belongs to us. Illness, accidents, grief, depression, all these passages make us remember, but only the better to shove that finitude aside; and it is really the eternity of presence that we settle for, that we play with, that we love. If this strange forgetfulness were to abandon us, if we were hurtled all at once into knowing exactly when and how we would die, what would become of desire? Philosophy cannot forget this, conceptualizing the world as it does back to back with death. Philosophy is a reminder of our mortal being; we have been trying our hands at it since ancient Greece. A civilization that thinks of being as not belonging to death, but that conceptualizes it on the basis of finitude, and forgetting. *Lethe.* And it is in that porous, fluvial forgetting—closer to hell than to purgatory—of our mortal condition that sex arrives. No appointment will summon it there, because it has already made this its business.

Sex is our only true response to the anguish of death. Making love makes us forget that life is always on the verge of ending and that the body itself belongs just as much to death as to life. Making love recalls us to death insofar as death is only conceived on the basis of life, and indeed that is what makes it always unreal to us; what fascinates us in death is its total opacity. Until the end we think within life, with death but outside of death. Sex holds me at the edge of the certainty that one day I will disappear. It puts beings in one another's presence and imbricates them, disimbricates them, but each time the energy that accomplishes this is blinding. It erases all other horizons but the one supplied by the bodies. For there to be ecstasy, everything else in the vicinity has to be coordinated with this plenitude, has to work with it. Words, obscenity, gazes are not enough; nothing suffices if there is not in the body an immediate absolute response to death. Copulating with cadavers was once a major crime, and the mere image of that act against nature enacted the crime a second time, in a way. Sex is the business of living beings haunted by the fear of no longer being present, of no longer being loved, the fear that nothing—acts, words, exchanges of all sorts—has been of any use. And this fear affects our dreams as well as our terrors. It may be that sex is our only response, then, an inaudible response, one never heard but begun anew in an endless merry-go-round that keeps us alive, desiring. And it may be that the joy that is discovered in this process is more intimate, more real, than our fear.

❧ ❧ ❧ Literature, Ever Again . . .

From this condition of mortality that destines us to sex and to thought, to this indefinitely postponed blind date between philosophy and the love of bodies, literature is born. But who will answer for that legacy? Sade summoned philosophers into the boudoir and no one was eager to accept; all of them, or almost all, made excuses, and even if a few did turn up, it was in haste. Among those few, Nietzsche kept company with Pascal and Kierkegaard, but the failure of their expedition is glaring. They said nothing, or next to nothing, about sex. Only the language that forged their texts was altered by it; this is called "style." They are our dinosaurs extracted from the bellies of fossils.

The term *blind date* speaks of jealousy, the light passing through *jalousies,* through half-closed blinds; it speaks of the blind person feeling his way; it speaks of the unimaginable meeting with "whomever," chosen by someone else—a meeting with someone with whom one cannot keep company, in any case. It speaks of mistaken identity and waiting: it speaks of the misunderstanding that will arise with the very first words, it speaks of sex and the words that surround it in order to avoid it, to obsess it, to put it in the wrong.

Here literature begins. With hunger and astonishment. With sex and love of knowledge fastened tight to the body. With desire and the whole history of philosophy in thin slices cut up raw.

The encounter will not take place. In other words, it has always already taken place in the two protagonists' lack of awareness, their failure to recognize that they knew each other (already), loved each other (already), had left each other and forgiven each other (already), and had finished, perhaps, with the fatigue of meeting. Of remaining only in the suspension of an unhoped-for encounter.

Literature is lost somewhere in the articles of this legacy. The legacy of a meeting that did not take place, for want of a witness, perhaps, a third party, an attentive friend who would have liked it to work out for them. No one to keep a vigil for us, finally, but ourselves, and for the rest we shall have to wait and see. This is how Kierkegaard put it, differently, ironically: "What philosophers say about reality is often as disappointing as the notice that someone spotted in a thrift shop: 'Ironing done here.' If a woman brings her laundry here to be ironed, she has been duped: the sign is for sale."

On the next sign, she might have read: "Sex and philosophy. Blind date in progress. Come in."

But she didn't look up. It was raining.

❧ ❧ ❧ No End

To be hungry (for the other).
– To be astonished (that the world exists).
Sex, cannibalism, philosophy, silence.

To desire, to think, to love.
This won't make a common world, but a language, yes, perhaps, so that we can be *in* that hunger, that astonishment,
   that love.

Notes

1. Ludwig Wittgenstein, *Tractatus logico-philosophicus,* trans. D. F. Pears and B. F. McGuinness, intr. Bertrand Russell (London: Routledge, 2001 [1921]), p. 5 (1, 1.13, 1.2, 1.21), p. 9 (2.1).

2. Ibid., p. 54 (5.43).

3. Lewis Carroll, *The Annotated Alice: Alice's Adventures in Wonderland & Through the Looking Glass,* ed. Martin Gardner (New York: Clarkson N. Potter, 1980), p. 89.

4. Baruch Spinoza, *The Ethics* (Malibu, Calif.: Joseph Simon, 1981), pp. 112–13 (part 3, prop. 2): "No one has hitherto laid down the limits to the power of the body."

5. Søren Kierkegaard, "The Point of View for My Work as an Author," in *The Point of View,* ed. and trans. Howard V. Hong and Edna H. Hong (Princeton, N.J.: Princeton University Press, 1998), p. 50.

6. Friedrich Nietzsche, *Twilight of the Idols, or, How to Philosophize with a Hammer,* ed. and trans. Duncan Large (New York: Oxford University Press, 1998), p. 55.

7. Plato, *Alcibiades I,* 133b–c, trans. W. R. M. Lamb, in *Plato,* vol. 12, Loeb Classical Library.

8. Plato, *The Republic,* ed. G. R. F. Ferrari, trans. Tom Griffith (Cambridge, U.K.: Cambridge University Press, 2000), p. 93 (3.402c).

9. Plato, *The Laws,* ed. and trans. Thomas L. Pangle (New York: Basic Books, 1980), p. 172 (6.783 a–b).

10. Aristotle, *Nicomachean Ethics,* ed. Sarah Broadie, trans. Christopher Rowe (Oxford and New York: Oxford University Press, 2002), p. 141 (3.12.1119b).

11. Ibid.

12. Plato, *Phaedrus,* ed. and trans. C. J. Rowe (Warminster, U.K.: Aris & Phillips, 1988), 254b.

13. *Heraclitus,* trans. Dennis Sweet (Lanham, Md.: University Press of America, 1995), p. 19.

14. Jacques Derrida, *Rogues: Two Essays on Reason,* trans. Pascale-Anne Brault and Michael Nass (Stanford, Calif.: Stanford University Press, 2005), p. 15.

15. Maurice Blanchot, *The Infinite Conversation,* trans. Susan Hanson (Minneapolis and London: University of Minnesota Press, 1993), pp. 53, 188.

16. Michel Foucault, *The History of Sexuality,* vol. 1, *An Introduction,* trans. Robert Hurley (New York: Vintage Books, 1990), p. 33.

17. Ibid., p. 34.

18. François Perrier, *La Chaussée d'Antin* (Paris: Albin Michel, 1994), p. 534.

19. Wittgenstein, *Tractatus logico-philosophicus,* p. 5 (1, 1.13, 1.2, 1.21), p. 9 (2.1).

20. Georges Bataille, *Eroticism,* trans. Mary Dalwood (London and New York: Marion Boyars, 1987), p. 23.

21. Immanuel Kant, *Prolegomena to Any Future Metaphysics,* ed. and trans. Peter G. Lucas (Manchester, U.K.: Manchester University Press, 1953), pp. 46–47.

22. Ibid., pp. 145–46.

23. Friedrich Nietzsche, *Thus Spake Zarathustra,* trans. Walter Kaufman (New York: Modern Library, 1995 [1954]), p. 324 (4.19.111).

24. Friedrich Nietzsche, *Unpublished Writings from the Period of Unfashionable Observations,* trans. Richard T. Gray (Stanford, Calif.: Stanford University Press, 1995), p. 198 (notebook 29, no. 20).

25. Jan Patočka, *Heretical Essays,* intro. Paul Ricoeur, trans. Erazim Kohák (Chicago and La Salle, Ill.: Open Court, 1996), pp. 104–5.

26. Ibid., p. 99.

27. Maurice Merleau-Ponty, *Phenomenology of Perception,* trans. Colin Smith (London: Routledge and Kegan Paul, 1962), p. 354.

28. Friedrich Nietzsche, *The Gay Science,* ed. and trans. Walter Kaufmann (New York: Vintage Books, 1974), p. 79.

29. Donatien Alphonse François, Marquis de Sade, *Français, encore un effort si vous voulez être républicains!* (Paris: Max Milo, 2004), excerpted from the fifth dialogue of *La philosophie dans le boudoir.*

30. Jacques Lacan, *Écrits,* vol. 2, ch. 1, "Kant avec Sade" (Paris: Seuil, 1966), p. 123.

31. See Jacques Derrida, *Of Hospitality: Anne Dufourmantelle Invites Jacques Derrida to Respond,* trans. Rachel Bowlby (Stanford, Calif.: Stanford University Press, 2000).

32. Søren Kierkegaard, *Concluding Unscientific Postscript to Philosophical Fragments,* vol. 1, *Text,* ed. and trans. Howard V. Hong and Edna H. Hong (Princeton, N.J.: Princeton University Press, 1992), p. 387.

33. Nietzsche, *Thus Spake Zarathustra,* p. 324 (4.19.12).

34. Annette and Gérard Haddad, *Freud en Italie* (Paris: Albin Michel, 1995), p. 25.

35. Wilfred Bion, *Taming Wild Thoughts,* ed. Francesca Bion (London: Karnac Books, 1997). I refer to Max Gaudillière's masterly seminar on Wilfred Bion, unpublished to date (Paris, École de Hautes Études, 2001–2).

36. Pascal Quignard, *Abîmes* (Paris: Grasset, 2002).

37. Plato, *Symposium*, 191a–b, 192a, trans. W. R. M. Lamb, in *Plato*, vol. 5 (Loeb Classical Library).

38. Peter Sloterdijk, *Sphères*, vol. 1, *Bulles: Sphères, microsphérologie* (Paris: Pauvert, 2001).

39. Charles Melman, *L'homme sans gravité: jouir à tout prix*, conversations with Jean-Pierre Lebrun (Paris: Denoël, 2003), pp. 112ff.

40. Frédéric Boyer, *L'ennemi d'amour* (Paris: P.O.L., 1995), p. 86.

41. Bataille, *Eroticism*, p. 23.

42. Blaise Pascal, *Pensées*, trans. A. J. Krailsheimer (London and New York: Penguin Books, 1995), p. 210 (fragment 638 from Lafuma First Copy edition).

43. See Friedrich Nietzsche, *Ecce Homo*, in *Friedrich Nietzsches Werke des Zusammenbruchs*, ed. Erich F. Podach (Heidelberg: Wolfgang Rothe Verlag, 1961), p. 273.

44. According to Pyrrho and the Skeptics, the philosophic quest has four possible states. The zezetic state is the moment of searching; the skeptical state is the state in which one finds nothing; the ephectic state is the search for a point of equilibrium and suspended judgment when the investigation proves to be unfruitful and the impossibility of establishing a universal order is discovered; the aporetic state is the final state of knowledge as doubt.

45. Spinoza, *Ethics*, pp. 112–13 (part 3, proposition 2, note).

46. Ibid., p. 74 (part 2, proposition 13).

47. Ibid., p. 87 (part 2, proposition 26, proof).

48. Ibid., p. 29 (part 1, definition 7).

49. Ibid., pp. 109–10 (part 3, introduction).

50. Ibid., p. 189 (part 4, proposition 37, note 1).

51. Ibid., p. 118 (part 3, proposition 9, note).

52. Ibid., p. 121 (part 3, proposition 15, corollary).

53. Ibid., p. 179 (part 4, proposition 19, proof).

54. Ibid., pp. 223–24 (part 5, proposition 4, note).

55. Ibid., p. 223 (part 5, proposition 3, proof and corollary).

56. See Steven Nadler's excellent biography, *Spinoza: A Life* (Cambridge, U.K.: Cambridge University Press, 1999).

57. Ibid., pp. 120–21.

58. Ibid., p. 130.

59. Ibid., p. 121.

60. Spinoza, *Ethics*, p. 208 (part 4, prop. 67).

61. Charles Malamoud, *Cuire le monde: rite et pensée dans l'Inde ancienne* (Paris: La Découverte, 1989), p. 117.

62. Jacques Derrida, "Reste—Le maître ou le supplément d'infini," in *Le Disciple et ses maîtres, pour Charles Malamoud*, ed. Lyne Bansat-Boudon and John Scheid (Paris: Seuil, 2002).

63. Jean-Pierre Winter, *Les errants de la chair* (Paris: Calmann-Lévy, 1990).

64. Jean-Paul Sartre, *Being and Nothingness,* trans. Hazel E. Barnes (New York: Washington Square Press, 1966), pp. 474–75, 477, 476, 480.

65. Franz Kafka, *Letters to Milena,* ed. Willi Haas, trans. Tania and James Stern (London: Secker & Warburg, 1953), p. 47.

66. Ibid., p. 85.

67. I refer here to their correspondence, indispensable texts published in Hannah Arendt and Martin Heidegger, *Letters 1925–1975,* trans. Andrew Shields (New York: Harcourt, 2003).

68. Lou Andréas-Salomé, *Looking Back: Memoirs* (New York: Paragon House, 1991), pp. 44–45.

69 Ibid., p. 47.

70. Ibid.

71. *Friedrich Nietzsche, Paul Rée, Lou von Salomé: Die Dokumente ihrer Begegnung,* ed. Ernst Pfeiffer (Frankfurt am Main: Insel Verlag, 1970), p. 110.

72. Ibid., pp. 125–26.

73. Ibid. pp. 129–31.

74. Ibid., pp. 153–54.

75. *Selected Letters of Friedrich Nietzsche,* ed. and trans. Christopher Middleton (Chicago and London: The University of Chicago Press, 1969), pp. 185–86 (cf. *Friedrich Nietzsche, Paul Rée, Lou von Salomé,* pp. 154–55).

76. *Friedrich Nietzsche, Paul Rée, Lou von Salomé,* p. 174.

77. Ibid., p. 175.

78. Ibid., pp. 175–76.

79. Andréas-Salomé, *Looking Back,* pp. 49–50 (cf. *Friedrich Nietzsche, Paul Rée, Lou von Salomé,* pp. 178–79).

80. *Friedrich Nietzsche, Paul Rée, Lou von Salomé,* p. 183.

81. Lou Salomé, *Nietzsche,* ed. and trans. Siegfried Mandel (Redding Ridge, Conn.: Black Swan Books, 1988), p. 78 (cf. *Friedrich Nietzsche, Paul Rée, Lou von Salomé,* p. 213).

82. A poem offered by Lou to Nietzsche on his departure:

> So truly loves a friend his friend
> As I love thee, O Life in myst'ry hidden!
> If joy or grief to me thou send;
> If loud I laugh or else to weep am bidden,
> Yet love I thee with all thy changeful faces;
> And should'st thou doom me to depart,
> So would I tear myself from thy embraces,
> As comrade from a comrade's heart,
> As comrade from a comrade's heart.

> With all my strength I clasp thee close;
> Oh, send thy flame upon me like a lover,
> And 'mid the battle's rage and throes,
> Let me thy Being's inmost self discover!

To think, to live till Time alone shall drown me,
With all thy floods my measure fill!
And if thou hast no bliss now left to crown me,
Lead on! thou hast thy sorrow still!

(Trans. Herman Scheffauer, in *The Complete Works of Friedrich Nietzsche*, ed. Oscar Levy, vol. 17 [New York: Gordon Press, 1974], pp. 209–14).

83. *Friedrich Nietzsche, Paul Rée, Lou von Salomé*, pp. 224–25.

84. Ibid., p. 256.

85. Ibid., pp. 261–62.

86. Ibid., pp. 262–63.

87. Ibid., p. 268.

88. *Selected Letters*, p. 198 (cf. *Friedrich Nietzsche, Paul Rée, Lou von Salomé*, p. 269).

89. *Nietzsche, Paul Rée, Lou von Salomé*, p. 279.

90. Ibid., p. 322.

91. Ibid., pp. 341–42.

92. *Nietzsche: A Self-Portrait from His Letters*, ed. and trans. Peter Fuss and Henry Shapiro (Cambridge, Mass.: Harvard University Press, 1971), pp. 78–79 (cf. *Nietzsche, Paul Rée, Lou von Salomé*, pp. 359–61.

93. George Steiner, radio interview in France.

94. Friedrich Nietzsche, *Human, All Too Human, I,* trans. Gary Handwerk, in *The Complete Works of Friedrich Nietzsche*, ed. Ernst Behler, vol. 3 (Stanford, Calif.: Stanford University Press, 1997), p. 12.

95. Jan Patočka, *Liberté et sacrifice* (Grenoble, France: Jérôme Millon, coll. Krisis, 1990), p. 36.

Name Index

Anne Dufourmantelle is a professor of philosophy at the École d'architecture La Cilette, Paris, and coauthored (with Jacques Derrida) *Of Hospitality*.

Catherine Porter is a professor emerita of French at the State University of New York, Cortland.

The University of Illinois Press
is a founding member of the
Association of American University Presses.

Composed in 10.5/13 Minion
with Caravan ornaments
by Celia Shapland
at the University of Illinois Press
Designed by Dennis Roberts
Manufactured by Sheridan Books, Inc.

University of Illinois Press
1325 South Oak Street
Champaign, IL 61820-6903
www.press.uillinois.edu